The Making of a Master:

Tracking Your Self-Worth

The Making of a Master:

Tracking Your Self-Worth

Jeanette O'Donnal

A Dandelion Books Publication
www.dandelionbooks.net
Tempe, Arizona

Published Worldwide
by Dandelion Books, LLC
Tempe, Arizona

A Dandelion Books Publication
Dandelion Books, LLC
Tempe, Arizona

Library of Congress Cataloging-in-Publication Data

O'Donnal, Jeanette
    The making of a master: tracking your self-worth

Library of Congress Catalog Card Number 2002117733
ISBN   1-893302-36-9

Cover and book design by Amnet Systems Private Limited,
www.amnet-systems.com,
"Stairway to Heaven" Cover art by Jim Warren Studios, www.jimwarren.com

Disclaimer and Reader Agreement

Reader Agreement for Accessing This Book

Printed in the United States of America

Dandelion Books, LLC
www.dandelionbooks.net

*I dedicate this book to the "I" that we all call "Me":
which becomes the "Master" of our destiny once
we awaken to the beauty of the "What" that
we all are—LOVE.*

Acknowledgements

First and foremost, I want to thank my parents for having nurtured within me a feeling of true freedom of expression as a child without criticism, and for having provided the arena for independent growth into the horizons of new thought.

I want to especially thank my seven beautiful children, each who have given to me a piece of the knowledge which I now hold as wisdom.

- My firstborn, Cami White, for her incessant verbal communication with me, which, throughout our experiences have awakened virgin territory in our search for answers to the mysteries of life.

- Danna Peil for her unending thirst for the information which we have researched together and independently, sharing our discoveries of uncharted territories.

- Spring Johnson for her critical eye and straightforward commentaries that have kept me steadfast and very aware of what I truly stand for.

- Raquel Williams for her never-ending application of the principles which we have discovered; and for her eagerness to share these "keys" with everyone she meets.

- Missi Hancock for her patient and pristine inner wisdom that has inspired all of us as family and all others who know her.

- Gordon Michael Peil, my only son, for his unending, trusting and unconditional love and non-judgmental attitude toward all of life.

- Cynthia Weishan, my step-daughter, for her steadfast trust in me to allow me to be one of her first teachers of the basic principles of a masterful life.

I also want to acknowledge the man who came into my life as "my fresh breath of air" at some of my most trying moments, Tom Taylor. Tom has supported me and given me the "wind beneath my wings" to cross over into new territory and detach myself from the dross of the past.

And I do not want to forget the great example of my friend Hal Ruegamer, who mentored me in the art of "standing up for myself" and putting into practice what had only been a philosophy of personal strength.

My great thanks to my silent "Sat Guru," my maternal grandfather, Manuel Galvez (Papito), for his great example as a Master. Even though he has departed from this world, he continues to be by my side as my silent guide.

I am extremely grateful to my many clients and friends who have shared aspects of their life with me; thus giving me the opportunity to use their stories as enrichment to my own story and the lessons this book imparts.

And to my publisher Carol Adler, I have reserved a special thank you for her sharp professional skills, her high publishing standards, and her optimism. Carol saw the potential in my writing for a tutorial book of rich principles for life. Thank you for your encouragement and prompt professional services as my editor.

The Making of a Master is a special initiation—your path to personal excellence and transformation of your heart.

Ancient Egyptians believed the wings of Ma-at (goddess of truth) represented the spirit of justice. The heart (*ab*) is where the emotional body (*ka*) and soul (*ba*) resided. For ultimate life mastery, these ancients were supposed to transcend beyond realms of physical existence through specific initiations that brought about justice and peace. When their heart, weighed against a feather (the symbol of truth), made the scales balance, they were to transcend into immortality.

In the ancient mystery schools, masters taught neophytes sacred truths. All initiates, including kings, queens, pharaohs, druids, priests, priestesses, chiefs, braves and chelas, received instruction and inspiration through initiation, consisting of spoken words, tasks, quests, chants, and meditations. They were given specific knowledge, motivating them to life mastery. They earned their transcendence by having lived a life of justice, truth and serenity.

If today you were to weigh your heart against a feather, would the scales balance? Personal excellence brings peace and tranquility, making your heart light. Once all judgment of self has been transcended, the reward is justice.

Preface

If you had to choose between asking yourself "What would I do to make my life better?" or, "What don't I like about my life?" which question would be easier to answer?

Like most people, probably you would be able to answer the second question in a matter of seconds. Usually it's easy to make a list of all the things in your life that you don't like and that you may wish to change.

The first question—What would I do to make my life better?—may take much more thought and effort to answer. Indeed, for most of us, it is easy to find fault with other people or circumstances outside ourselves, and far more difficult to create a plan for making personal or internal improvements. Witness the time and effort it takes for a child to build a castle with blocks. Then, one push from the tiny fist of another child (circumstances outside ourselves) is all it takes to make that carefully constructed tower topple over!

It is no coincidence that you picked up this book and have decided to read it. Obviously, you are ready for a meaningful change. It is also easier than we think, to make those changes. My dear friend, Jean Warner, puts it beautifully in her book, *Messages From The Light:*

> Many seek to discover their purpose for being. Some feel they are here to learn. You are here to experience, not to learn that which you already know. But remembering what you know—in particular, who you are—will help you to know experientially rather than just conceptually.

In other words, you are a work in progress; but the only "work" involved is to allow yourself to be open to experiences that will deliver information about "who" you are and why you are here. Sitting in the bleachers and watching the game of life going on around you will not give you those answers. You must get right down there in the playing field and get involved.

You are about to embark on a new and exciting adventure. Perhaps it will be the most important journey you have ever taken in your entire life, because it will help you to experience what you may already conceptually have understood but have not yet "actualized" or put into action.

In this book I will share many ancient secrets with you, basic principles which I will call "keys." It seems that no matter how well we may intellectually "know" these concepts, often we fail to use them. Indeed, it's as if these principles are so easy, we can hardly believe they will really open the doors to greater happiness, self-fulfillment and personal excellence!

Please feel free to share these principles with others.

Key # 1 - The way out of where you find yourself today is through the same door that brought you here.

That door is you! And regardless of how you may have judged your past experiences, they are what brought you to where you are today. You will discover how each experience has served as a stepping stone to your dreams. You will discover: 1) how to wholly embrace every experience, and 2) how to vividly feel your dreams ... you will become your dreams.

You will be amazed by your inner power to make changes that will produce everything you desire.

Does this sounds magical? Well, you *are* magical!

There's a saying that if you want something strongly enough, you will get it. That "wanting" is a feeling so strong, it is often called passion.

Do you really want to make changes in your life? Are you absolutely certain that you're ready for a new adventure?

Key # 2 - Experience teaches in a lifetime what passion can teach in an hour.

Passion for life is what you are about to realize. This does not mean abandonment of reason or common sense in the reckless pursuit of pleasure. Rather, it is a feeling that bathes your entire being with delight. It is a true "knowing," through and through, that you can be and do and have whatever you desire.

Life is a gift of nature. What we do with that gift—how we use it to create a peaceful loving existence, is something all of us can do—if we want to. In time, we receive a second gift as a reward for applying what we know. That reward is the earned gift of wisdom.

Contents

Introduction

"To LOOK is one thing,
To SEE what you look at is another.
To UNDERSTAND what you see is a third.
To LEARN from what you understand is still
something else. But to ACT on what you
Learn is all that really matters."

— Malcolm P. McNair

Many years ago I experienced what has been labeled by mental health professionals as depression. I felt emotionally drained and in a slump. I didn't seem to be interested in doing anything. This was very unusual for me, since I was a person with a lot of zest for life. My days were always busy and full, but now suddenly I didn't feel like doing much of anything except sleeping.

I was unhappy about this state of mind, mainly because I felt so unlike myself, so lazy, and incompetent. What was causing my unhappiness—my feelings of lack?

In order to answer that question, I knew I would have to ask another: What would truly make me happy? That was easy, I told myself at that time. Money—lots of money to buy myself the things I desired. I am a hairdresser, so I set to work more diligently at my profession. This seemed like a sensible approach.

It took a few rides on the merry-go-round of life's events for me to discover how wrong I was about the "Money Equals Happiness" equation. Neither the job nor the money I earned seemed to have anything to do with my state of mind or how I felt about myself and my life—my lack of true freedom.

Like most people, when I started to have a few unresolved problems, I found myself caught up in the nasty cycle of asking, "What went wrong?"; "Where did I take the wrong turn?"; or, "Where did I make that first mistake that made me do this?"

Eventually I discovered a far more effective and powerful way to solve my problems, turn my life around and earn my personal freedom. It is this method, "Tracking Your Self-Worth," that I am going to share with you in this book. I will give you the "keys" that unlock your magnificent self within. I am going to show you how you can become happier and more fulfilled than you ever dreamed could be possible.

If you now find yourself in a slump, asking "What went wrong?" this book will map out a new course of action that will by-pass these and other negative, often destructive self-interrogations.

I'm sure you know about the human brain's ability to receive and process messages. However, what you may not be aware of is that when you ask of yourself "What went wrong?" your mind responds through a series of impulses, by researching the disk-packs of the brain for an answer ... some way to resolve the problem.

Key # 3 - *Focus on the joy you are attempting to achieve and the self-gratifying reward will be happiness.*

When you ask yourself "What went wrong?" your mind will be unable to come up with an answer or resolution to turn you around, because there is none. Instead, just the opposite happens. The outcome of your brain's research for something "wrong" triggers self-sabotaging attitudes that remain hidden from the conscious mind. These attitudes often destroy our efforts to resolve the real issue because we are caught up in self-judgment.

Hidden agendas, in turn, result in creating circumstances that bring self-inflicting punishment. As this weapon takes over it appears to be correcting the problem of what you have called "wrong." It is this type of behavior we must stay away from in order to create self-worth.

My friend Shannon was caught up in a life of self-sabotage. "Life is rotten. It's just not working out the way I want it to," she'd complain. Her complaints often became a litany. Since we worked in the same beauty salon, I became accustomed to hearing stories of her divorce and how horribly her ex-husband had treated her.

She'd whine about unappreciative clients and the many other people in her life who had mistreated her. Eventually I shared my tracking method with Shannon, and as she started to catch on and use it to assess her self-worth, soon she came to find value in the trials she put herself through.

Shannon kept asking herself, "What went wrong?" and calling herself "stupid" instead of asking with great feeling: "What is right?" or, "Why did I create this situation?" or, "What am I to learn from this experience?"

Soon Shannon started to be grateful for the people who had come into her life who had given her opportunities to grow and change her attitudes and perceptions. Searching for the answers to "what is of value" will trigger your brain to start loving yourself. It will initiate the process of self-discovery, self-honesty and self-love. This jump-start will give you more pleasure than you can imagine. Almost magically, your life will start to turn around.

Chapter 1

Know Yourself

*"For some people, listening to their consciousness
is like taking advice from a stranger."*

— Author unknown

Eventually I learned that happiness, fulfillment and freedom don't just come along one day. Rather, they are something we grow toward. They are what happen when we act differently after having awakened to a forgotten knowledge.

Before we can learn how to track our self-worth, we must begin the journey of self-knowledge. On this journey, we will start to become acquainted, at the deepest soul level, with that "I" or "I am" that is the subject of the "me" that we are tracking.

What does it really mean, to know oneself?

I remember my grandfather asking me when I was thirteen: "Do you know who you are?"

I wanted to give him an impressive answer, but all I could manage was: "Well, I know you know who I am, so I'm assuming you're looking for an answer that both of us don't know!" That may have seemed like a clever reply, but deep down I knew I wasn't fooling my grandfather—or myself.

The drive—passion—to understand ourselves can make us into inquisitive human beings. It can even lead to personal growth—which is why you are reading this book. You have come to that time in your life when curiosity is getting the best of you.

Or, maybe you are driven by self-disgust, another big self-knowledge motivator. That's okay too. Sometimes our most negative, unwanted feelings act as a trigger for moving us forward. All of our feelings are valuable and serve an important purpose in our growth.

It doesn't make any difference how you arrived at this point in your life. What really matters is that you are here. You have found yourself asking The Big Question: "Who am I?"

This question is usually followed by another: "Where can I find that door I can walk through to find out?"

Key # 4 - The magical door to self-discovery is not outside somewhere, but "within."

The third question surfaces: "How do we access our self-discovery?"

Value Yourself

To know ourselves, we must be able to highly value ourselves. Also, we will want to value ourselves.

This doesn't mean we have to become vain or conceited. The best way to describe what it feels like to value oneself is to remember those precious moments of childhood when you felt happy. It was a feeling that told the world, "All is well. I feel how alive I am! I am filled with energy and enthusiasm, zest for life."

Robbie used to come every month like clockwork to get a haircut. A commercial advertising agent for a local newspaper, she always looked her best and made sure she was on time to all of her appointments. Robbie talked upbeat; her vocabulary was well polished. She never seemed to experience a moment of discomfort in spite of the pressures of her job and the urgencies of her life as a mother of two little boys and a baby girl She seemed to have her both her professional career and domestic responsibilities under control.

In the ten years I knew her—before she moved out of state to accept a better position—Robbie was friendly and pleasant. She had a great sense of humor and never spoke ill of anyone. Her type of work certainly exposed her to some complaining faces, but Robbie always spoke of her customers as dear and loyal to her. Robbie had a knack for knowing herself. Wherever she went, she exuded that inner connectedness.

"It's rather simple," she'd say. "Just keep things simple, and life has a way of working things out."

I was sad to see Robbie leave for Connecticut, but with an attitude about life like hers, Robbie was well on her way to always finding success and happiness, regardless of where she lived.

Without self-esteem, we can't possibly feel like Robbie. So ... what do we need to do in order to acquire this precious asset? It's easier than you think.

Self-Love

You've heard about the magic of love. How about self-love? Self-esteem begins with self-love. Okay, but how do we start to love ourselves? What do we need to do?

When you were a child, do you remember how much fun it was to swing your arms around without touching anything? Just swinging and swinging. Or possibly you liked to spin like a top—knowing you would not be bumping into anything. Freedom to move. Freedom to breathe. Freedom to be you. Freedom ... and joy ... There was a happiness in knowing you were free.

We seem to be isolating words, but still, we don't know how to "get" freedom, "get" joy ... and thus, "get" self-love.

Not long ago, my daughter Spring, who is now 29, was having a severe case of hives. She had applied a variety of methods to help in the healing process; she had spent a large amount of money going to Mayo clinic for advice and medical attention.

Spring was desperate. Nothing seemed to work.

What she was not paying attention to were her deep-seated feelings of disappointment, resentment, rejection and loneliness. She felt misunderstood and therefore not very happy about herself. Spring had lost touch with her divine spark. She was withholding her words of love for herself and others. Her body was displaying the results of a diseased attitude.

Then she discovered the power of forgiveness.

Key # 5 - Self-healing can easily be achieved through the power of forgiveness.

Through the act of forgiveness for herself and others, Spring soon awoke to freedom—her own power to heal herself and regain self-love. She discovered that unpleasant memories of the past, making her feel guilty, sad, angry, remorseful and depressed, were not useful to herself or anyone else.

Forgiving herself and actually expressing and feeling self-love finally brought true healing and relief.

When you are at peace you are joyful; when you feel loving inside, your whole being responds joyfully.

Key # 6 - Forgiveness is the key to freedom, joy and self-love.

Explore your past for guilt, fear, remorse, resentment, anger and other hurtful issues you may be harboring against others or yourself. "For" + "give" = forgive-ness: the giving of yourself, or surrendering of your unwanted feelings, thoughts and actions.

My dear client, Kelly, had spent many hours talking to me about how her father had sexually abused her and how this had fostered hatred for her father. It took a sincere and deep look within for Kelly to come to forgiving herself and her father.

Kelly took time to discover who she really was. Reflecting on her feelings opened a gateway for self-love to come through. Willingly and lovingly, she began to respect and understand herself. This self-knowledge bore fruit in the form of forgiveness toward her father. Kelly's inhibitions healed and her relationships with men improved. She was more assertive in her work and soon gained a major promotion in her area of expertise in the financial world.

Victor or Victim?

Often we tend to create situations that seem to put us in the role of victim. When we seriously investigate the source of many of these problem-situations we discover we have let ourselves get insulted or hurt because we have not forgiven ourselves. It may take an accumulation of many painful incidents for us to come to recognize our strengths.

Taking responsibility for our own actions opens the door to self-respect, joyful results and ultimately, freedom.

My co-worker and friend, Jennifer often said she had a life full of "bad luck." Often she talked about the bad men she had married and divorced, or she would complain about the nagging bosses who had caused her to quit her job and move on to yet another nagging boss.

Eventually, like my friend Shannon, Jennifer found forgiveness; but not until she was able to recognize her unwillingness to stop defending her point of view and insisting that she was "being picked on."

Jennifer also had to start valuing herself and stop giving her power away to others: husband, boss, the driver who didn't signal before turning left, the salesperson who shortchanged her . . . the chocolate chip cookies that insist she eat not one, but a dozen. When you blame someone or something else, you empower them. Then you become the victim. Defending herself and arguing with others was holding Jennifer back; she perceived herself as trapped.

When I worked with Jennifer, sometimes it was difficult for her to understand what I was saying about the rewards she would experience by taking an earnest look at her attitudes. However, once she made this self-evaluation a routine, allowing time for this special self-attunement, her life came into balance.

Key # 7 - Keeping life simple can be effortless.

The flow of your life will be smooth when you make conscious efforts to maintain relationships that are uncomplicated. What do we mean by "uncomplicated"? Simply put, keep your conversations straightforward. When you make clear statements with no hidden meanings or agendas, you will rejoice in the peace and harmony you will experience. Ulterior motives destroy clarity of communication and soon chisel away at simplicity.

My youngest daughter, Missi, who is now 26, had a relationship with a young man, Aaron, who was interested in her. It wasn't long before she discovered that his conversations seemed to have an ulterior motive. He was willing to agree with her philosophy of life intellectually but his actions indicated otherwise.

Aaron would be willing to go to the movies or the restaurant selected for the evening, but if, for example, they had difficulty finding the place, Aaron would become irritated and expect the same response from Missi. By nature Missi is a happy person who keeps things simple. Such small things didn't bother her. When Aaron saw that she didn't share his irritation, he would begin to pout, acting unhappy or indifferent.

Missi found this behavior emotionally exhausting and eventually elected to end a relationship that was causing both of them to lose respect for themselves and each other.

What Missi gained from this experience was a confirmation that she should continue to keep her life simple and honest, in open communication with others.

As a child, do you remember playing with butterflies, trying to catch them as they fluttered from flower to flower? Do you remember wishing to be a kite up in the sky on a windy February day so you could fly like them? Keeping life simple makes one feel light as a kite and just as flowing.

Key # 8 - Letting go of the past refreshes the present moment.

Escaping the slavery of our past is like entering the game of real life without baggage. In order to break away from this bondage we have ignorantly chosen, first we must assess what is useful in our present life and discard what no longer serves the purpose of self-worth.

Like children who sometimes fail to look before they run into the street, too often we plunge into the next experience without releasing this baggage. We find ourselves "stuck" in the past and closed off from the path to freedom.

What does this baggage from the past look like? Here are some examples. Possibly in your earlier years, one of your parents used to call you stubborn, or lazy, or messy. The label stuck and since that time you have believed yourself to be stubborn, lazy or messy. Your current behavior may reflect one or more of those characteristics.

A teacher may have told you that you would never be a good math student. You have had problems with math ever since. Your mother maintained you would never be good at ballet, so you never pursued the dream you once had as a little girl. Your parents favored your brother or sister over you and when they passed away they did not remember you in their will, leaving the house, summer home, boat, cars, stocks and bonds to the other sibling. You still harbor anger and resentment against your parents, and jealousy toward your brother or sister.

Your dog was killed in a car accident and you blamed the driver. You still hold that grudge.

Feelings of hatred, resentment, remorse, guilt, loss—any type of negative feeling or feeling of lack depletes our precious energy.

Key # 9 - Acting as if, even if it is not actually so, brings results in time.

If the best you can do at this time is pretend that you're happy, that's okay. It's perfect, in fact. My sister-in-law Elena always said it this way: "Fake it till you make it." Remember the song that says "... just put on a happy face ..."?

When I met Robbie I wondered where she was coming from with her big friendly smile. Was she faking it? It didn't take me long to determine that both Robbie's smile and her attitude were genuine. Robbie is an example of someone who used the "as if" method: "Fake it till you make it."

Shannon, Jennifer, Spring and Missi also practiced happiness until it started to come to them more naturally. First, however, they had to release unwanted emotions from the past. By genuinely loving themselves (practicing forgiveness) and keeping their lives simple and straightforward, they no longer needed someone else to "cheer them up." They stopped blaming themselves and empowering others.

Say "No" to Self-Denial!

Can you be truthful, frank, and friendly with yourself—or do you try to find excuses for your attitudes and behavior? It took time for me to able to cut through all the self-blame and rationalizing that had become a solid layer of protection from growth, and freedom.

When I started to be honest with myself, I also stopped being afraid to express myself. I no longer cared what others might think, feel or say. I was who I was, and I began to accept and admire that "me."

Key # 10 - How you feel about yourself is how you will appear to others.

If you feel happy, self-confident, joyous and in sync with your life, this is the message you will deliver to others. They will want to spend time with you, just to experience your radiance, and your positive attitudes and outlooks. As a child, every moment of life was joyous; I radiated that joy. But as I grew older, layers of self-blame started to cover up that free-flowing sense of being in sync with my life. Before I knew it I was depressed. It was like paddling a canoe that was surely sinking.

The holes in my canoe were caused by past feelings of lack or loss, in turn caused by anger and other unwanted emotions. Once I released my anger and started to sincerely love myself, my joy returned. It became fun to patch the holes in my canoe.

After my divorce 20 years ago, I attended a community class called "Divorce—Starting Anew." In this class I applied some of the things I had discovered about myself. I began to express myself in a positive way, in spite of the negative circumstances I had endured. I was more friendly and less resentful.

I actually made a conscious effort not to bring up my past as a "victim of circumstances." Simply and without emotion, I would explain my situation, as a loving and understanding woman who was ready to face the single world again. Through this class, I gained many new friends and lasting relationships. At the end of the six weeks, I discovered it was not my incredible story that surrounded the circumstances of my divorce that drew students to me, but my positive attitude and sense of self-worth, self-respect and freedom.

With these "keys" to open the doors to your inner power and freedom, you will easily glide into your new adventure. You won't have to look back again at those outdated attitudes that served their purpose in getting you here!

Starting to Track

Below is the first set of tracking questions. You may wish to write down the answers in a journal that you will keep from now on.

Remember, you are releasing all traces of self-judgment. There are no "right" or "wrong" answers. Simply read the question and without too much hesitation, answer with the first thought that flashes into your mind.

Tracking Questions

1. What single word best describes your state of mind at the present moment?
2. Can you remain silent in spite of your desire to react in an argument?
3. What are five ways that you value yourself highly?
4. What six obstacles stand in the way of your joy?
5. What two times in your life can you remember when you felt uncomfortable among people who were different from you? Did you need to defend your point of view?
6. What four things will you change about yourself to gain more self-worth?

Tracking Exercises

1 List ten characteristics that you feel are presently a part of your self-worth.
2. Give five examples of how you have taken personal responsibility for your actions to create a win-win outcome.
3. List six occasions when you have felt the "light" within you has been in command of your decisions.
4. List four examples of your ability to express yourself in a "neutral" manner toward someone who demands self-defending responses for their comments. For example, your responses could be, "It's interesting that you feel that way." Or: "That is a very creative way of looking at it." Or, "Interesting creation!"

5. Make two columns, one with the heading, "What went wrong?" and the other with, "What am I to learn from this experience?" Then review your answers as they pertain to five situations in your life.

6. Commit yourself to six new ways of looking at your life with a new attitude. List these six ways. For example: "I will find at least one constructive reason why this has happened to me"; or: "When my brother says something that triggers a contrary feeling inside of me, I will stop myself from insisting I have to clarify myself to him." (His comments are his personal issues.)

Chapter 2

Building a Successful Now

"Enthusiasm is one of the most powerful engines of success. When you do a thing, do it with your might. Put your whole soul into it. Stamp it with your personality. Be active, be energetic, be enthusiastic and faithful, and you will accomplish your object. Nothing great was ever achieved without enthusiasm."

— Ralph Waldo Emerson

Regardless of the dead-end appearance of many situations in your life, you do have the ability within yourself to establish a successful outcome. When you have acquired the strength to begin the willful process of your change, you will have the courage to succeed.

If you begin with an optimistic attitude and a liberal dose of enthusiasm, you will soon discover that success is not a resting place but a process to be enjoyed. This enthusiasm brings great opportunities.

Growth may at first look overwhelming to you, but in reality any change that you make delivers another stepping stone toward developing integrity and dignity.

Key # 11 - Enthusiasm gives you the perspective necessary to reach a balance.

An enthusiastic look at any situation already makes you feel successful. But intentions are merely ideas unless you apply them. How do you begin?

13

How does one become enthusiastic? How does enthusiasm help us recognize opportunities for growth in our daily life?

Confidence Creates the Foundation

Confidence has been defined as a childlike outlook. In his book, *Creative Living For Today*, Maxwell Maltz, M.D. F.I.C.S. writes about how to make every day an exiting experience: "You remember the confidences of your past successes again and again in your mind, seeing them and smelling them, until they become part of you."

Key # 12 - Seeing it in your mind is like having it!

Once you establish a memory vivid enough, you will recall former occasions when you felt self-confident and assertive. Recalling these feelings will bring you to a state of inner balance. The process of remembering is often called centering, or "going within."

Many people take time every day to center themselves. They may have a special time and place where they sit quietly or meditate, freeing their mind of everyday mundane thoughts and allowing themselves to become one with their inner self, or being. It is my experience that this special time allows the self to return to its equilibrium, or state of balance.

Magically, once you achieve this state of balance, you find yourself filled with renewed strength and courage. You feel as though you could meet any situation, any challenge with the "courage of a lion" even when you feel like a cub. Instant confidence prepares you for success.

My dear friend Wilda had come to Arizona to visit me from Pennsylvania; she was after some "R & R" in the sunshine. Wilda had undergone an operation for breast cancer and was feeling tired and weak after the chemotherapy that was administered.

Recently, Wilda had attended a special retreat where she learned about concepts for changing her attitudes. Wilda wanted to begin implementing these in her daily life. While visiting together we talked about ways to grow and change, and we began a process of remembering many of our happiest moments from the past.

Before long both of us were laughing at experiences we had almost forgotten. With great confidence and enthusiasm we were able to regain our balance—and freedom. Once more we felt as though we could easily and joyously meet life's challenges.

By the time she was ready to leave, Wilda felt like a new woman. She had re-charged her batteries. I felt enriched for having spent precious moments with her.

Establish a Plan of Action

Human beings are creatures of habit. We tend to follow automatically those pre-recorded patterns established by previous experiences. It is true that experiences afford us knowledge that we may use as a powerful tool, but this knowledge is useful as power only in its rightful context and clear focus.

For instance, your knowledge about mathematics will not be useful for choosing a loving mate; nor would your patterns of behavior while attending a Catholic mass be appropriate for scuba-diving.

In order for you to be able to use information acquired through experiences, you will need to examine yourself to establish just how much information you really have about what you are pursuing.

Key # 13 - Being certain about what you want creates the energy to materialize it.

Once you have determined what it is that you want, with passion you can proceed with a plan. You must begin with a definite plan of action and direct it to a definite end. After you have the image of what you want—a direction, in your mind—confidence establishes the foundation. Enthusiasm combined with self-confidence are the keys that unlock your power.

Give Yourself Permission

Key # 14 - In order to be successful, you must first give yourself permission to use this freedom.

Why do we sometimes refuse to give ourselves the liberty to exercise the enthusiasm that releases powerful actions? Many times it is the fear of not being accepted, or perhaps the worry that we will do things wrong.

Sometimes it is simply lack of direction that keeps us from moving forward. I am reminded of my friend Alan, a bright amiable person, who appeared to have the necessary potential for achieving his goals in life. Yet he never seemed to reach that peak or finish line. Why was this so? I asked myself. Alan was always there to help others. For his friends and relatives, he had tremendous amounts of enthusiasm. Yet when it came to meeting his own challenges, his attitude radically changed. Gone was the excitement; gone was the confidence that comes from inner balance and a sense of connectedness.

If you have your plan of action in place, you will have no trouble moving forward with your dream. "The choice is up to you," continues Dr. Maxwell. "You must utilize the worthwhile creative instinct within you to succeed—not fail." Give yourself permission to begin something new. Begin your plan of action by writing down your feelings in a journal. Then you will have a map to follow.

It is when you begin to feel desperate or overwhelmed that you start to lose ground.

Key # 15 - Worry is a nasty worm that thrives on enthusiasm.

When you are worried or afraid, the worms come out to play. Whenever you feel that worry worm crawling into your enthusiasm and confidence, shift your energy, fast! Shine some light on that worm and make it crawl back into its hole. Smile, even if you don't feel like it. Act as if you are enthusiastic, and you will be. Remember, nothing has the power to overtake you unless you allow it to do so.

"Most fear today is psychological," says David Schwartz, in *The Magic Of Thinking Big*. "Fear is success enemy number one. Worry, tension, embarrassment and panic all stem from mismanaged, negative imagination."

Again, just think: "I can!" and the magic will take over.

Key # 16 - *It's the little things that count.*

To enjoy success in the future, heighten your feelings and enjoy the little things of life that make life exciting, right now. RIGHT NOW is your moment of power. Make the little things in the NOW the most important events of your life. Once you learn to "live in the now" you can count on having bliss for the rest of your life.

Key # 17 - *Your limitations are only what you believe them to be.*

When you adopt the motto: "Success comes in cans and failure comes in can'ts," you'll look at fear with self-confidence and humor. Believe you can have it and it is yours!

Open yourself to new experiences. If at first they feel uncomfortable, give them some breathing room without getting into judgment. Remember, judgment is different from assessment. It's okay to check the water level of that swimming pool before you jump in. In fact, it's a good idea to be cautious and check out the details of any situation before taking action or making a commitment.

On the other hand, you can spoil the joy of any experience by telling yourself the water is too cold or the thrill of the dive is okay for some people but will never be fun for you. Feel great!

Key # 18 - *Feeling great every moment keeps you centered.*

"You feel good not because the world is right, but your world is right because you feel good," says Vernon Howard, author of *Psycho-Pictography: The New Way To Use The Miracle Power Of Your Mind.* Keep checking yourself against your plan of action in your journal. How are you doing? Do you feel optimistic? Do you have fear of loss, lack or limitations?

When you find yourself in the presence of another individual who chooses to display behavior that does not show respect toward self or others, how do you feel? Do you start to feel queasy in your gut?

Be aware of the way other people's actions make you feel, and where you feel that uneasiness in your physical body. If it is an issue of love or lack of it, you may feel it in your heart. If you sense that people are not listening to themselves talk and their words are harmful or hostile, you might start to hear a roaring in your ears.

Remember: You don't have to participate in their drama. Remove yourself and stay in your own state of inner peace and happiness. No need to get into the stuff of others. Use those experiences as a point of reference for yourself. Another way of saying this is to use these encounters as a time to assess how you are feeling rather than judging the actions and behavior of others. Stay happy; be detached!

My son, Gordon, now 21 years old, has a natural ability to remain happy, even in the midst of chaos and disruptions. He also has a knack for quickly recovering from any dilemma that might have caused him worry or concern. When he was less than two years old he became physically unable to maintain his balance. He fell often, scraping his knees and scratching his face.

Gordie did not allow this temporary physical handicap to interfere with a cheerful disposition. He did not use it as an excuse to be bitter about life and he didn't let the worms of fear or distress start to eat at his happiness.

Key # 19 - When you are happy with yourself it is easy to be happy with others.
The height you reach in life—your altitude—depends in great measure upon your attitude. When I was learning how to

fly an airplane, my instructor always said: "The attitude of the airplane is where the nose of the craft is pointing (ascending if pointing upward and descending if pointing downward); thus the altitude of the craft depends on its attitude."

Our daily experiences are manifestations of what our mind harbors; they are a "hard copy" print-out of our thoughts. Therefore, it is of prime importance to have an attitude of hope, courage and self-trust.

Set Your Attitude to Positive!

When you think about something long enough, it will manifest in the physical world. The events you bring into your life are the outcomes of your thoughts. These thoughts are neurological connections that become "memories." They deliver information or data to the mind, which then processes it.

These "memories" are imprinted data that produce images for the physical reproductions of these thoughts. The brain passes no judgment upon the input; it simply accepts it as knowledge. Positive thoughts are seeds of courage that have germinated in your imagination. Our experiences are the results of those thoughts.

Key # 20 - Know that you are free to create the world you wish to experience.

This is called free will. You are totally responsible for your thoughts, feelings, attitudes and their outcomes. When you feel the slightest emotional discomfort toward anything, let it be a clue that you are in a state of judgment. Discomfort is a "check yourself" signal for you to go within. Ask yourself why this situation is affecting you. A maser will make an assessment without judgment or emotional involvement.

One time when I found myself feeling uncomfortable about the way a mother would scream at her unruly children in the supermarket, I asked myself what was causing this feeling.

My inner self responded readily, telling me I was witnessing a prime example of the Golden Rule. If I were that mother screaming at my child, I would be in judgment toward myself.

This little exercise of going within whenever I felt discomfort about any situation has taught me how to be not only accepting of others' behaviors, but understanding and loving as well.

The principles that you continually contemplate as your thoughts are the determining factors of your outcome. The winning edge in every aspect of your life comes from a focused determination and a healthy mental attitude. These are the first ingredients of the formula to self-realized freedom.

Respect for self and others is the second ingredient of this formula. Since our physical body is the instrument or "holder" for our experiences, it is the respect we have for our physical bodies that initiates a respect for others.

Your attitudes influence your state of mind. Those attitudes you feel more strongly are the ones that occupy your mind most frequently. Therefore, the easiest way to maintain self-respect is to keep yourself in a state of self-awareness. Be conscious of your attitudes. Monitor or track them, and self-respect will follow.

Keeping an optimistic attitude is the third ingredient of this formula. Fear and worry produce unwanted stress signals in the physical body. "Thoughts are always associated with subtle and not-so-subtle emotional feelings," says Richard Restak, M.D., in his book, *The Brain Has A Mind Of Its Own*. He adds, "That's because within the brain the areas mediating thoughts and feelings are interconnected." For example, when you wake up happy, your whole day manifests a disposition of joy. On the other hand, if you choose to wake up feeling pessimistic and the whole world looks gray, your day will be filled with doom and gloom. Most likely most of the day's events will manifest themselves in a negative way.

I'm reminded of a story of two widowed twin sisters who lived together. Both were writing a letter to their children about their Sunday afternoon. One wrote about the beautiful snow that glistened outside their window and the angelic sound of the children's choir that morning at church. She also was pleased to have been able to bring a pie to their neighbor who had been ill.

The other twin complained about the dangerous drive to church because of the snow and how noisy and disruptive the children had been. She wrote about the neighbor's miserable state of health and complained about having to bring her food. "It isn't easy to give, when you have so little yourself," she wrote. She was right; she had little love to give and it surely wasn't easy.

Key # 21 - Your outcomes will match your attitudes.

When you decide to experience life with an optimistic and enthusiastic attitude, you can count on sunny, fun-filled days, and the bonus of almost more zest than you can handle!

Opportunities sometimes look like obstacles. An enthusiastic optimistic attitude helps you stay relaxed and friendly, regardless of your circumstances. Tension may not melt away, but you will deal with it differently. You will look at obstacles in your life as opportunities.

Most often you will find something good in your relationships. You will adopt habits, such as listening to soft music or reading from a book of wisdom, taking a few moments to gaze out the window at the garden or trees, or the birds chirping and twittering at the feeder. Or you may enjoy the austere silence of the sun rising over the mountains. You may take time to play a motivational tape that is especially inspiring. Or maybe you will sing in the shower. You will associate with people who are optimistic and fun to be with.

Quickly and easily you will find solutions to your problems. You will have a wonderful time living in the Now!

Seven Steps to Activating Your Success

Here are seven steps to follow in order to establish a foundation that will serve you in building a moment-to-moment successful life. Begin every day using these simple steps and you will discover a more fulfilling life and a winning attitude. I suggest you copy these seven steps on a sheet of paper and tape them on your refrigerator or some other place in your home where you cannot miss reading them several times, every day.

Step # 1 - Be conscious of your thoughts. Be selective. Think only about those things that feel good and produce enthusiasm and successful outcomes. Success is not a magic pill but the result of conscious effort, every day, every moment of your life.

Step # 2 - The words you speak are energy forms reflecting your thoughts. Build your conversations with the intent of expressing exactly what you wish to experience in your life. Your thoughts, which are your beliefs, become your words and create your realities.

Step # 3 - Act like the person you wish to be. By taking the responsibility of deliberately creating your outcomes, you release your enthusiasm and confidence and manifest your desires.

Step # 4 - Remove any beliefs you have that scream out: "Lack!" "Loss!" and/or "Limitation!" These are beliefs that produce fearful experiences. Fear depletes your creative energies for success and accumulates worries that eat away at your self-confidence.

Step # 5 - Regardless of what situations may look like, always live your present moment in bliss. Having the courage to work things out gives you the strength to experience your life in success. Don't be overcome by impatience. Things are not as they seem. Maintaining enthusiasm brings magic into your life.

Step # 6 - Begin each day with the attitude that everything is perfect, exactly as it is. The power behind this belief lies in your nonjudgmental attitude. The scriptures say, "Ask and it shall be given." So, ask for what you want!

Step # 7 - Stop defending your point of view. Defending your point of view simply tells others that you are seeking approval and desire to control situations that you have judged as not having been in your favor. When you have complete self-confidence you don't need to be defending the direction you have chosen to follow.

The Canvas of Life

On this wonderful canvas each of us is given, we can be supreme artists of life by creating experiences that bring us happiness. The secret of enjoying a life of peace and harmony, of achieving that state of bliss where all is well no matter what happens, is to know without a doubt that we have the ability to create whatever brings us the outcomes we prefer in any circumstance—and that we are still in a state of grace with ourselves and the world.

The magic lies in knowing where you are going, having a way to get there—and enjoying the journey along the way.

Questions for Discussion

Remember, there are no right or wrong answers to these questions; the first impulsive thought is usually the answer that will give you a truer picture of where you are. Do not debate too long over any question or statement.

1. Are you happy with what you are now experiencing on a regular basis?
2. What do you wish to change? Explain briefly.

3. What does enthusiasm mean to you personally?
4. How does your present behavior reflect your mental attitude?
5. What are some of the little things in your life that mean a lot to you?
6. Do you often find yourself defending your point of view? Why or why not?

Follow up with these Exercises

1. List five things you propose to do to help you in developing self-confidence.
2. Make an outline of the plan you'll use to stop defending your point of view.
3. List ten optimistic attitudes you plan to practice every day.
4. Make a written plan of how you have carried out enthusiasm in the last two days.
5. Make your own drawing of the motto: "Success comes in cans, and failure comes in can'ts."
6. List three methods you will use to get yourself out of an uncomfortable situation in which someone else is being disrespectful.

Chapter 3

The Magic in Your Thinking

*"Whenever I am successful I know I have chosen,
consciously or unconsciously, to use the positive
thoughts that have created my success."*

— Spencer Johnson, M.D.
The One Minute Sales Person

Key # 22 - Manifested life is a fallout of our thinking.

Manifested life is nothing more and nothing less than the transformation of a thought into the physical, much like the process you go through as you stand in front of a vending machine ready to make a selection. Your thoughts would be like the offered items, passing through your internal vision for you to choose. You make a selection, push a button and your item drops down for you to claim.

Although it may seem like magic to those who do not understand the technology behind this machine, it is nothing more than an imitation of the natural process we use for obtaining anything we desire. When you mentally reach out to touch a thought, like the item you have selected in a vending machine, it will drop into your life as the experience you will now have, or live.

Many of us do not realize the power of our thoughts. In truth, if you really know what you want, it is not difficult to "push a button at the vending machine" and get your selection. But sometimes we're not sure exactly what we want. The choices blur. As a result, some of our experiences are not necessarily those we think we may have chosen.

We may not know we pushed that "unwanted" button that produced a life experience that caused us pain or unhappiness. Why did this happen to me? we ask. How did I bring this (stress, frustration, misfortune) into my life?

Perhaps we really didn't know how powerful thoughts can be. When you know what it is you want and you understand the process of how you create life's situations, you will no longer be taken by surprise. Be assured, there is great power in what goes on in your brain; handle with care!

The delightful magic is not only in knowing exactly what it is you want, but in *making sure you focus on it*. It's just as easy to think about what you don't want; so be careful!

Fears Are on the Rampage

Key # 23 - When fears are on the rampage we create more of what we fear.

Remember the saying: "That which you fear shall come upon you"? Why do you think this is? When you have a fear you actually spend considerable time thinking about that fear—and when you think about it, you give it power. I'm sure you have experienced this phenomenon.

Too often, we really don't know what we want—or we don't know we really are capable of deciding. Those who scatter our energy, giving power to other forces, never really getting what they say they want, are generally the same people who complain a great deal and are quick to say that life treats them unfairly.

Did you ever think about the fact that you empower the people, things and circumstances that you blame?

When you remove the veils of confusion and complexity from a string of complaints, the culprit reveals itself. Call it indecision, or lack of focus. Indecision is a decision not to decide. Indecision is a form of fear.

Under all the rubble of indecision lurks what I call a transparent belief—a thought to which you have attached disruptive emotions and stored in your subconscious.

Key # 24 - Transparent beliefs are bearers of unhappiness.

Since many beliefs are transparent, we cannot see them; we actually chose subconsciously not to see them as powerful influences in our life. Why would we do such a thing?

Martin Sussman, founder of the Cambridge Institute for Better Vision, believes that emotional disturbances such as financial failure, a career change, the loss of a loved one, may cause unawareness of underlying forces that affect our lives. This is why sometimes we are surprised at what we are manifesting and experiencing, often erroneously blaming others. More on transparent beliefs a little later; first, let's see how we begin to create them.

We start to perceive ourselves as victims. Others are making us miserable. Others are causing us to fail.

I'm amazed at responses people give when I ask: "What do you really want?" Melissa answered, "I never thought about it." Anthony said, "I don't know why I don't know."

Note a child for a moment; it took Kimberly only a second to give me her answer: "I like puppies better than cats, that's why I got Bootsie for my birthday." Children always know what they want! This is why they manifest their wishes. Unencumbered, focused and persistent, they charge their desires with enthusiasm, which produces almost instant manifestation. That is also why they often believe in magic. Why wouldn't they?

How to Discover Your Desires

To find what you truly want to be or do or have in life, you can start by looking at the obvious areas in your life where you like to spend your time. These may be your hobbies.

Most people have at least one activity to which they give their focused attention because it is an enjoyable activity. For some of us it may be a sport. For others, it could be reading a book. Going on a hike might be the ticket for another. Where do you find yourself most often? Do you like to shop for home decorations? Do you spend a lot of time poring over certain magazines ... or in your garage reconstructing a car engine? Perhaps you find yourself at the computer playing games. Do you shop for collectibles, antiques, or specific craft items?

The answer to these questions will usually convey what you most often think about. Some may find themselves spending a good portion of their time at the neighborhood tavern with drinking buddies, or at the doctor's office, waiting to deliver a long list of symptoms that will probably lead to more prescriptive drugs, another operation or still another specialist to visit. Or they may find themselves sprawled out on the sofa, watching television. Does this exercise deliver a powerful message?

Yolanda came to my shop one afternoon, disturbed about not having enough money to pay her rent on time. Recently she had been ill and had missed several days from work. Her supervisor reminded her that this was the last time she could get absentee pay, since her record showed she had missed too many days already. Yolanda blew up at her supervisor and was given her walking papers.

She had been looking for work and couldn't find anything, she said; but from her comments I discovered she could have had several jobs. Yolanda had chosen not to take those other offers because they were not what she really wanted to be doing. "I'll never be a nurse's aide; they could never pay me enough money to push a cart around for them sick people!" Or: "I could never see myself sitting at a desk all day and answering the phone." I quietly thought to myself: "She could at least have made enough money to pay her rent this month and then start to look for work she would enjoy."

Yolanda had created a situation that she thought was unfair: fired from her job, not enough money for rent, bad job offers ... the list goes on. The part that Yolanda failed to see was that her own thoughts were bringing about the circumstances in her life.

Some find it easier to look at the things they don't enjoy doing in order to come up with an obvious clue that will help them decide what they truly prefer. Try this yourself. Start by listing the things you dislike. How does it make you feel, focusing on the negative instead of the positive? Does it seem to attract grouchiness, depression, tiredness, and a whole host of other unwanted symptoms? You may find yourself actually manifesting situations you dislike, just like Yolanda.

Thinking about negative things also causes stress; it causes one to feel depleted. Does it seem easier to understand why, in this frame of mind, focusing on negative thoughts, you will manifest what you most wanted to avoid? Are you getting the picture?

Let's place our energies on the experiences we want to have.

Make It Easy on Yourself

At the top of a sheet of paper, write: **"Things I Want to Gain, Attain, Accomplish or Be,"** and start your list of preferences. Call them your desires or your dreams. Make things simple and enjoy the process. The sky's the limit! Loosen up and notice how much fun you can have.

Johnny knew how to follow through with his dreams. One day while he and his mother were out for an afternoon ride, his mother stopped the car beside a beautiful field of wild flowers. Johnny jumped out of the car and picked a large beautiful bouquet for his mother. He knew exactly what he wanted to do the minute the car stopped.

You don't have to be a child to capture the spirit of childhood.

When I see that my pursuits are getting complicated and stressful, I will have an internal conversation with myself: "Let's bring my present situation to its lowest denominator

(I call it "lowest denominator" because I dig to the bottom line) in order to determine what direction I really want to go with it."

For example, I look at the motivating factor that got me to commit to certain activities such as working long hours or accepting a dinner invitation when I would rather stay home and rest or read. These unwanted situations often result from fear of loss, lack or some limitation that we are experiencing at that time. We believe this fear will be alleviated by engaging in these disruptive or unwanted activities.

I remember when I was in college I accepted a movie invitation from a former boyfriend. I really was planning to finish reading a book required in one of my courses. I didn't want to go but I also didn't have the courage or assertiveness to refuse. By accepting the invitation, I let myself down. It is experiences like these in retrospect that have served to bring awareness into my life.

I've discovered that asking myself to dig within for the motivating factor—asking myself what I am doing and why I am doing it—helps me to balance and then focus on choices I prefer. It also allows me to make changes quickly.

It boils down to keeping my life focused and simple, and continually seeking more knowledge to overcome my ignorance.

Free the Runway for Accomplishment!!

Key # 25 - If you free your life of emotional obstacles you will make room for accomplishments.

You will find yourself scattering your energy unnecessarily if you move in too many directions simultaneously, without having first chosen what it is that you really want. Decide on one thing and move on it. The dwindling away of precious energy by the suffocating habit of being afraid to commit to one direction only causes more convolution in your life.

Making alternative plans always splits your energy of focus. Worrying about making the wrong decision because you have done so in the past, and being afraid of making changes, also adds to the stress.

Let go of the negative—all those "what if's"—and simply make that choice. Deep down you really do know what you want—so go for it!

"What could be so fatal?" I always ask myself.

When you don't decide what you want and focus on that dream, it's like attempting to plug up the leak in your canoe by hammering nails around a patch. Each nail hole makes another place for the canoe to leak.

First become more aware of your thoughts because they will reveal the direction you are already on. Deciding what it is you want and where you want to go—what you prefer to experience, becomes easier.

More on Transparent Beliefs

Transparent beliefs are primary motivators that you are unable to detect. These motivators may cause you to make decisions that lead to situations you would prefer not to experience.

Similar to the lens of a camera which causes the picture to appear closer or farther away or a different color than it really is, transparent beliefs cause your expected outcomes to emerge differently. Remember the vending machine? Something has made it malfunction.

At some point, you have acquired these beliefs and they continue to affect your experiences. Lodged in your subconscious, they are like "stuck" energy that you cannot detect because you may not even know they exist.

How to Identify Transparent Beliefs

Let's say a person desires to be wealthy but may not know about the transparent belief, "I am poor," that is stuck in his subconscious. This transparent belief delivers a picture of poverty and creates a roadblock for the wealth wish to manifest itself.

We could give a similar example for the person who really wants to have a slim, shapely body. A transparent belief, "I'm ugly if I'm not slim," or "I'll never look like him (or her)" will keep that person from getting their wish. Other more complex subconscious transparent beliefs could be attached to the outcomes of the wish. For example, "If I become slim, I will want to buy lots of clothes, and I don't have money to buy clothes." Or, "If I become slim, I might attract a man or woman who wants to be intimate with me. I've been through that before, and it surely hasn't worked in the past. I don't want that to happen to me again. Never again! I'd rather hide out in my fat body!"

Not until the person heals that inflamed transparent belief, will the true desire freely surface. Overweight individuals must dissolve the belief that they are fat, unworthy or limited in some way, and then they will shed those unwanted pounds. Transparent beliefs can be destructive and deceiving.

Remember: when we voice a desire we are stating that we are "in want" of it—in lack of the very thing we are desiring; get it? The key here lies in the intelligent fine-tuning of the desire. *You must propose the desire as a dream that you wish to experience and not as a lack of something.* Only the attitude, not the wish, changes.

For the person who wishes to be financially wealthy, the dream truly lies in the desire to have something more. It does not relate to the lack of money or financial resources. But if you ask that person about their wish, you will discover their deep agony is due to the feeling of lack. They do not have the childlike feeling of want for the sake of having.

You may also notice that these people usually desire something that is connected to a hidden agenda. Possibly the Williamsons next door have a new SUV and they still have a three-year-old van. How does it look to the neighbors if they can't also buy a new car? The Williamsons belong to an expensive country club; all the "right people" belong to that club. They need more money in order to belong, or fit in, or impress others.

Now let's take a good look at those individuals who think they are "fat" and want to be "thin." These people have hidden agendas of comparison. For example, the overweight person will look at another overweight person and feel disgust. Thus, they create the same feeling about themselves, since they are comparing themselves to that overweight person.

Another universal twisted belief sounds something like this: "Food makes me fat"; "I'll get fat if I eat that"; "I'd better stop eating so much ... I'll gain another ten pounds"; or, "I ate so much on this vacation, I have to go on a diet and lose five pounds by the wedding."

The transparent beliefs behind all of these attitudes about food are numerous. Everyone has their own reasons for saying what they say. But their own emotionally attached attitudes from past experiences cause the fallout of thoughts that produce what they are living. The statements they made have become their reality.

Do you know someone who continually talks about wanting to quit smoking? If they have not been successful thus far, they may have a transparent belief that keeps playing out: "I will get fat if I quit smoking," or, "I'd rather smoke than be fat." Or it may deliver the message, "I'm not worthy of being a person who doesn't smoke."

It might even be saying, "I hated my grandmother who used to smoke in my face as a child, and I'm getting back at her because she didn't want me to smoke."

These hidden beliefs are sometimes buried under much "baggage." The attitudes we assume toward others, in maligned judgment, also bear the truth to our own transparent beliefs.

Search out your hidden destructive emotionally charged motivators and stop creating what you would rather not experience.

It takes time to become aware of our most disruptive patterns of behavior that lurk in the shadows of our past. But I can tell you from my own experience that it is well worth the effort. How would you like to go up to a vending machine and look at pretty colored packages and not know what they were to deliver to you once you selected them? Transparent beliefs are just like these mystery packages.

Neutralize Situations that Steal Your Energy!

Key # 26 - Some situations rob you of your calm; neutralize them.

Only we can determine to stop stress before it begins. My friend Roxanne decided to attend a marketing seminar in Colorado, and after one seminar session, she discovered she was not enjoying herself. She was restless and bored and most of the participants had come to the resort to gamble and drink. Roxanne did not enjoy either of these pastimes, so she decided to take a side trip to a ski slope.

It was the height of the season, and Roxanne did enjoy skiing! She had a marvelous time breathing the invigorating air and enjoying the elegant mountains. She did not regret her previous decision to go to the seminar; she simply turned her attention to what she would prefer to be doing and released the stress this experience could have caused her.

Roxanne discovered she had a transparent belief—that either she did not deserve to spend the money to treat herself to a ski trip in Colorado, or a ski trip to Colorado was too expensive. But guess what? Her real desire won out over her transparent belief! She listened to her inner self and asked, "What do I really want to be doing right now?"

Release, Allow, Trust and Evolve

Key # 27 - Once you release the past and allow the present to spearhead the future, trusting in the divine power within, you will evolve much faster.

The cause of many sorrows stems from sentimental attachment to circumstances that aided in the making of initial decisions—"stuck energy." One example is the way we first fall in love. If that relationship ended bitterly or on some negative note, we judge ourselves harshly, blaming ourselves for the outcome. We carry this emotional burden with us into the next relationship.

Not until we completely release that heaviness, can we walk light-footed. The experiences we create for ourselves are passing dreams—they are adventures. Enter every adventure with a clean slate. You don't have to let your past experiences haunt you. If worry comes out to play, shine your light on it. Develop an inner peace that remains unruffled by the situations of this life. Keep your focus on the things you prefer to encounter and hold an attitude of trust. Charge forward—in one direction. Make life more fun.

When you have a stressful situation, follow these steps. I call them:

5 D's of Creative Thinking

1. Discard it: Be done with whatever is bringing you stress. Stop bringing up the emotion.
2. Date it: Set a definite date for resolving it.
3. Detach from it: Stop perceiving it as important. Neutralize it without becoming upset.
4. Deal with it: Face the facts and do the best you can to resolve it.
5. D.R.E.A.M. with it:
   Diet properly—do not begin a binge or a starvation diet.
   Relax. Take a bubble bath or rest leisurely in a hammock.
   Exercise and think of solutions only.
   Align with your self-worth.
   Motivate yourself to creating the dream you prefer to experience.

Changing Your Mind is Not a Problem

Key # 28 - Changing your mind is not a problem; so, stop punishing yourself for doing it.

When changing your mind about anything, begin by asking yourself: "What could be the worst scenario if I change my mind now?"

The purpose for change is to create a more peaceful life. The courage to make any change requires a non-judgmental attitude toward yourself. Changing your mind does not indicate lack of self-worth, nor is it a stamp of incompetence and irresponsibility.

Key # 29 - Avoidance is an indication that other people usually have something to do with your indecision.

If you cannot bring yourself to an awareness of what you prefer, you must determine if you are simply avoiding this "knowing." Avoidance is an indication that other people usually have something to do with your indecision.

This attitude reminds me of Lana, who came into my beauty shop one day to get her hair cut. She wore a smile but had a heavy heart. Lana was struggling through the loss of her job, much like Yolanda. But Lana had already gotten past the sad face; she simply needed more information to get herself out of the "victim" mode. Her brother had encouraged her to go after the firm that had employed her, with a legal attack for discrimination. Lana didn't want to put herself through a long drawn-out legal fight.

She asked me what I would do in her case. I only had one answer: "What do you want to do?"

I encouraged her to determine if it was her desire to go to court or if this was something her brother had wanted her to do. Lana was feeling like a "victim" of not only her unemployment but of her brother's suggestions. Once Lana took the courage to change her mind and stop being the victim, her own decision came readily. She chose to move on past the experience and use it as a textbook for future employment experiences.

Don owned his own business but was having difficulty finding dependable help. In the process, he began to lose faith in himself. His self-confidence plummeted and he couldn't decide how he was going to manage without help.

When Don told me about the situation he also asked me how I would recruit dependable employees, since I was an employer myself. I shared with him some of my ideas. Sitting in my haircutting chair, Don learned not only how to gain reliable employees but also some concepts for tracking self-worth.

I didn't have to say it; he realized that he was trapping himself in a "needy" attitude. Soon Don reversed not only his attitude but his employee situation. He spent his energy doing what he most liked, and the creative energy started flowing. It didn't take long for him to have all the happy employees he needed. Don realized that changing his mind and releasing his victim consciousness would open the floodgates to success.

Once Lana and Don had recovered their strength, determined what they wanted and found worth in being self-respecting human beings, they were able to represent themselves, to themselves, authentically.

My friend Betsy, who loves to garden, is one of the examples I use in my self-worth classes to show others how easy it is to change your outlook about any situation, find what you prefer and discover your worth.

Betsy loves flowers, so she spends many hours outdoors in her garden. She told me that time with her flowers is time for herself. It is in these moments that she sorts out "baggage" and gets rid of those things she prefers not to live with in her comfortable life style.

Betsy says: "It's like pulling weeds. I choose what I want to keep in the garden of my life. I bring my color of the rainbow into the picture and all the rest I simply admire, like I do my flowers."

Key # 30 - When you are able to hold a dream—a passionate desire—in focus, it is easier for the universal forces to deliver what you desire.

It's simple; you need only to desire it strongly, and it will be there for you. It is only the complexity we bring into our lives that keeps us from experiencing the bliss we prefer. Deepak Chopra, one of my favorite spiritual authors and teachers, often talks about living in bliss. Manifesting your dream can be simple, but it does require strong focus and acknowledgment of the great power within.

The Magical "As If"

Key # 31 - Living "as if" is truly living the magic of your power within.

Live like the thought has already manifested your desires. Remember, the greatest manifestations come from the imageless "want."

Nobel Prize physiologist, Charles Robert Richet, wrote, "Because a fact is rare is no reason that it does not exist." Another great mind, Sri Yukteswar, a Jhanavatar Guru of Paramahansa Yogananda said, "Imagination is the door through which disease as well as healing enters. Disbelieve in the reality of sickness even when you are ill; an unrecognized visitor will flee."

It is that simple. The obstacles come from our outdated minds. Let's take courage from these great minds and forge along into our new path.

Abolish the slightest trace of fear. A ship in a harbor is safe, but ... that is not what ships are built for. Henry David Thoreau said: "In proportion as he simplifies his life, the laws of the universe will appear less complex. If you have built castles in the air, your work need not be lost; that is where they should be. Now put foundations under them."

Knowing and trusting the magical power within to give you what you want is a great foundation for building your castles.

What Blocks Progress?

I know it can be difficult to change your outdated belief systems; many people will object: "You must be realistic!" or, "Don't kid yourself!" You may have to get used to your new ways of thinking, your new skill of selecting your thinking.

Key # 32 - Strong feelings are the key to manifesting your dreams.

Emotions are tricky; they can also block your progress. A noted neurologist and Ayurveda expert, David Simon, M.D. lists several emotions that produce disease in human beings: fear, frustration, rage, resentment, hatred, envy, and jealousy. These are forces caused by the thoughts that have triggered the endocrine system to produce harmful chemicals or hormones. The repetition of negative messages and release of harmful chemicals block a person's progress. Ultimately, as Dr. Simon noted, they will produce disease.

The only antidote that can save people from being destroyed by these powerful destructive forces is love. We have called love an emotion also, but in reality it is an energy that bathes the entire body with bliss—it is a virtue.

The manifestation of love in your being is not the result of chemicals produced by the human body's endocrine system, triggered by the thoughts you selected. Love is the natural peaceful state of simply being!

Live the Truth of Your Dreams

Veronica lived by herself in a college town; I had been her hairdresser for several years and had talked with her about the secrets I'm sharing with you now. Veronica wanted to establish a strong relationship with one of the bachelor professors. She was having a difficult time bonding with Carl. They dined and danced together but something was still missing for her to feel more bonded to Carl.

When she allowed herself the risk of being vulnerable, she began talking about her deepest feelings. She permitted herself to share with him some of the concepts we had talked about.

Previously, she had felt a university professor would be critical toward her. However, to Veronica's joy, sharing some of her emotionally charged feelings helped Carl to understand her better. He also felt more valuable to her in their relationship when he talked her deepest truths. Veronica told him how she had discovered and released some of her transparent beliefs. She had been self-conscious about her former weight problem, and she told him about her struggle—and victory, the loss of 45 pounds.

Through Carl's feedback, Veronica realized she had started to live the truth of her dreams. Carl also opened up and told Veronica about his own human foibles and how he had dealt with them. Thus began a deepening of their relationship.

Veronica also realized that she had started to experience life with a passion. She had set goals for herself, kept her focus, and removed the blocks that kept her from achieving her goals. Talking with others about your new-found knowledge to others also strengthens the impact.

Key # 33 - Evaluating your progress after initial application of an idea is imperative to the establishing of a habit.

Monitoring changes is valuable to progress as you begin the journey within. Remember, having skills is one thing; to use them in the process of developing your character is yet another. As the famous Dr. Maeser said: "A man without character is a ship without a rudder."

Your Brain is the Engine to Your Success

Scientific studies show the brain builds neurological connections for the purpose of improving memory by linking new concepts to what we already know. Since it is easier for neurological connections to run through already created paths, it requires focused practice to get our neurological paths to create new connecting stations for building memories of new concepts. The focus, therefore must be on those thoughts we truly wish to experience.

Key # 34 - If we are to change outcomes we must also replace established attitudes with those we have determined are ready to supply the energy we are after.

The integration of two neurological connections makes it possible to create a new concept. Recognizing thoughts that automatically cross your mind and taking the time to jot them down will enable you to begin a more automatic personal change engine. Thoughts profoundly affect your mood as well as your interpretation of an experience. As we stated earlier, thoughts trigger the chemical response in your endocrine system that will cause you to feel the results of your thoughts.

Thomas Fuller, M.D. said, "Seeing is believing, but feeling's the truth." Ask yourself: "What do I prefer to feel and experience?"

Notice the amount of time you spend entertaining certain thoughts. I have had successful results by taking an appointment schedule sheet and tracking my thinking processes by jotting down my thoughts at the appropriate times on the schedule.

In my self-worth classes I've asked my students to track themselves from the moment they start their day, and to continue as diligently as possible to jot down the general idea of their thoughts until they are ready to go to sleep. Usually in a matter of three days at the most, every one of them has located the places where they encounter difficulties.

They are impressed by their own thought patterns and enthusiastic about the changes they quickly resolve to make. Check your own thought patterns. Watch how they will silently create a graph of your life. See how they have set the patterns of your activities. The great fun comes when you make alterations in your thoughts and experience the magical changes in your life!

Pay Attention to Your Intentions

Key # 35 - Experiences take you where you want to go.

You are in the driver's seat. Since experiences are initiated by your thought processes, by necessity they carry an intention or motive.

Intentions are creations of the mind. They are created by the silent choices we make with the accumulated knowledge we have within. Outdated motives got you in trouble when you did not yet know yourself or had not determined your self-worth. You are now beginning your new journey of self discovery— paying attention to who you may have been acting like—and realizing who you really are!

You will enjoy tracking your thought processes and discovering the "essential" you! When you harness a thought (push the button) and recognize the motive, you will begin to be in control of your life. Because actions that follow your thoughts produce exactly what your intentions direct, you must place your self-worth where you wish to experience it. Become aware of your thoughts. This enables you to have a high quality outcome. *Pay attention to your intention.*

Check Around; Find Who You Hang Out with

Key # 36 - Conversations and relationships are a result of our thinking.

Our actions reflect our intentions and our words deliver our thoughts. Of necessity we must begin a process of gleaning the thoughts we wish to keep and discarding those we no longer prefer.

Retain only those that are in favor of your dream. Every thought carefully selected determines reality and brings about the treasure of life called joy! When you have joy you are self-realized—or is it the other way around?

Contentment screams out that you are in love! You hate no one when you are in joy. You love yourself! You also know who you are. Wisdom to know yourself comes from self-worth through tracking your magical thoughts.

Key # 37 - *Your words are the building blocks to your experiences.*

Take note of the time you spend talking about what you don't want, because your words are the building blocks to your experiences. If you find yourself not liking what you are experiencing, this is an indication that something is in need of repair.

The vending machine may be out of change or out of product. Or possibly it's taking the money and not delivering the goods. Listen to your internal conversations. What you are saying is what you are getting! You'll be surprised to find how indifferent you have been to your speech and the words you select to use in your conversations.

The way you look may be the "attention getter," but the way you sound is the "attention holder." Your physical appearance is telling others of your mental attitude; but, your voice and choice of words will reveal your internal position—your self-worth. And the image you deliver begins with attitude. For instance, if you tell yourself you are insecure, that is the message you will deliver. Once you have made a change in your language and "speaking attitude," you will be surprised at how it affects your situations in life.

Another factor involved in the outcome of our life's experiences is the way we talk about ourselves. Talk as if you are already the person you dream to become. Remember, your actions will reflect your words. Delete the transparent beliefs and stop kidding yourself.

My daughter Cindy had undergone eye surgery; this caused her eyesight to be impaired so I drove her to her doctor's appointment. With my assistance, she was walking from the car to the office, talking and acting as though she were blind. I suggested she evaluate her attitude. She quickly threw her shoulders back and spoke with the determination of a strong healthy person. Her recovery was swift and her self-worth remained intact.

Like Cindy, who turned around her attitude and began to act like the person she wanted to be, we can all give up being "blind" to the world we wish to experience.

Key # 38 - *If a thought can cause an intention, a thought can also turn it around.*

Consciousness upon which our intentions feed does not judge. Neither does it keep score. Remember, intentions come from the soul's agenda. The soul's single purpose is its evolutionary existence—its expression.

Our awareness develops as a result of our improved self-worth. Take a good look at what you might be overlooking. Is your life exhibiting what you prefer to experience? Have you become blind to your dream?

Don't feel bad about having let yourself down at some point. Guilt becomes another weapon to use against yourself. It is so easy to fall into that trap.

Ken is a nice fellow. He's a good-looking well-built guy with a friendly smile. One factor Ken had overlooked was his attitude toward women. He always chose to be with great-looking girls who were fun to be with. As a result, he found himself in a repetitive and uncomfortable pattern of spending time with girls who were desirable to other men. This caused him to become jealous. Ken was punishing himself by using others to create a victim role for himself. Do you see the twisted messes we get ourselves into? In our ignorance we weave these webs and trap ourselves. Our transparent beliefs stand in the way of our clear vision. Ken only needed to feel good about himself as the best candidate for the woman he was dating, rather than the fall guy who was going to be eventually dumped.

Key # 39 - Becoming passionate about the outcome of our life causes us to develop more creative ways to relate to others.

Make it your conscious choice to create more joyful experiences! Build a foundation of self-confidence and then build your dream upon this foundation. Release yourself from relationships that do not support your dream, and chart a new journey.

Becoming passionate about the outcome of our life causes us to develop more creative ways to relate with others. Be exceptionally loving and kind toward those who are experiencing your changes. They will have outbursts of retaliation and misunderstandings. "What is happening to you?" "You are falling apart!" "You need to be more realistic!" "Stop denying your emotions!"

You will receive many comments like these, just as I did. You must be firm and stay strong! Be careful to disengage from others' comments without criticizing them. Remember, everyone has their own realities to live out. Each of us has our own reasons and karmic causes for what we do and say. They are not wrong; you are not right. Everything is working out in harmony and divine order.

You are on your way to improve yourself in a loving way. They may need time and more knowledge to understand you and themselves in the "bigger picture." They also need a loving hand; share this book with them.

When you are acting and living your dream as it is materializing, you will notice how easy it is to make choices. Remember, many who are in your circle will criticize you. You just have to have the fortitude to allow it to come to fruition. No one else is creating your life. This is your show— and your opportunity!

Time Is an Illusion; Use It To Live in and Then Move On

Key # 40 - One of the most common stumbling blocks to a simple and blissful life is the conditioned belief in time as a reality.

Because our ancestors gave considerable importance to the division of time into segments—dividing time into past, present and future, they invented precise instruments to measure these segments. This gave them a frame of reference. Measurements of time became a basic element of our existence. It didn't take long for us to forget that we were measuring an arbitrary factor that was merely an illusion.

You may find yourself becoming impatient about your progress if you use units of time to measure it. Edward Witten of the Institute for Advanced Study in Princeton commented that the old theories of space and time may be "doomed."

Physicist Nathan Seiberg, also of Princeton states: "I am almost certain that space and time are illusions." With these comments from leading scientists, it is safe to say that the present moment is where your power lies; or, the Now is all that truly exists.

Time is only a succession of hours and events called chronology. "The history of physics is the history of giving up cherished ideas," says Harvard physicist Andrew Strominger. For lay persons and physicists alike, the hardest ideas to give up are those outdated notions of space and time.

Our memory enables us to be conscious of the passing of time. We can retrace the course of our existence and the experiences we have had along the way. We might believe that events closer to the present are easier to recall. However, current experiments and perhaps our own experiences will prove otherwise.

I have explained earlier that the power of recall is linked to the interest we take in the events we wish to remember, and their emotional impact. Our interest in these events depends on our power of concentration at that moment. You might recall fact$ dating back to your childhood and yet be totally unable to recall recent events.

This phenomenon demonstrates that our memory does not retain time, thus proving it is indeed an illusion. The imprints that remain more vividly in our memory are those which have been created by our strong emotional conscious participation. *Therefore, what really matters is our conscious participation in the experiences we are creating.*

The passing of time is not the important factor. Time only allows the space for the experience to take place and "imprint" the memory. It is imperative to challenge yourself to becoming more conscious of your thoughts, because it is these thoughts that will produce your feelings, ultimately leading to behaviors, habits and actions. Thus, our successes will bring about more successful experiences.

In his book, *About Time: Einstein's Unfinished Revolution*, P.C.W. Davies states that at the completion of his research and investigation, he was just as confused about time as the reader will be, after reading his book. In *Taking the Quantum Leap* and *Parallel Universes*, physicist Fred Allan Wolf expresses in lay persons' terms, modern discoveries that have been taught for millenniums by the masters, yogis, gurus and avatars.

When we lose all notion of duration, we become masters of time. Only through the development of transcendental meditation and other methods of metaphysical practices can we easily overcome illusions of time. Projected dreams, for example, are not measured in the same dimension of time, because time is an objective state of consciousness. This is how you are comfortably able to act like you have already built your dream home, for example, even though it is still in the planning stages.

When we stop looking for obstacles and overcome the effects we bring upon ourselves by negative emotions involving time—impatience, resentment, fear, worry, disappointment, frustration, boredom, irritation, hostility, hate, anger, anxiety, and grief—we will enthusiastically grow closer to our hearts' desires. Then our dreams will be free to materialize. All we need to do is transcend the self-imposed limits of time. We become the lion that once was a cub.

Knowing that within our deepest self lies the real world of Cosmic Eternity causes us to sail upward on a downward stream. Within us is the light that will dissipate all shadows and bring forth the magical realization of our dreams.

You will soon discover that cosmic forces will effortlessly present circumstances that will allow you to test your new knowledge and ability to realize your deepest wants. Wisdom—knowledge plus experience—will soon become your prize jewel.

It seems ironic sometimes to know that we can easily make some things happen. We create certain dreams within a short period of time. Yet, when it comes to other things, we seem to be at our wits' end.

When we plan a trip we can be very efficient in obtaining plane tickets, packing our bags, getting ourselves to the airport and arriving on time. But when we have a bitter argument with our spouse, we seem to forget how we can pull ourselves out of the mess we created by our emotional outburst.

Planning a wedding has more favorable results than planning a divorce. Why do you think that is? We create a desirable image in our minds, and bang! The outcome is automatic. Note that plans that we view with desired outcomes are not encumbered with barricades. Plans with less favorable outcomes such as the results of a dispute with a loved one or permanently separating from one with whom you have shared loving moments, triggers emotional (endocrine/hormonal) judgments and attitudes. These serve as impediments, causing a whole host of destructive emotions such as anger, fear, resentment, regret, etc.

Know what you want to achieve as your end result. Find "role models" and learn how these people have created their results. Study their habits and behaviors; listen to what they say and how they say it. Always include your "role model" within.

Refrain from Self-Defense

Key # 41 - It is not necessary to defend your point of view.

Once you have acquired the habit of evaluating your life without mental and emotional attachments you can enjoy the sweetness of your earned blissful state. Be humble yet proud of your accomplishments by harnessing your inner wisdom. Even if you may not agree, sit and listen to others express themselves without insisting on presenting your viewpoint.

Also, it is not necessary to defend your point of view. Your inner composure will reflect your wisdom.

Chelsie had a 14-year-old son who was confronting her about the house rules she had set for him. Chelsie simply and lovingly stated that she had set the rules in order to maintain respect and harmony in the home. If he obeyed these rules, his reward would be a car when he was old enough to get a license.

Her son, like many teenagers, pushed the issue. Chelsie did not defend her point of view but insisted that her son respect her rules. After several bouts of anger that did not make Chelsie yield, the boy began to look closely at the reason for the rules. He realized that his future as well as his mother's and other members of the family would be affected if he chose not to obey them. Chelsie was proud of herself as well her son, once he came around.

You will be surprised to learn that as you take these "baby steps" toward changing your life and ordering it to manifest your dreams, you will start to activate a universal power. Know that we are the natural recipients of this power. Listen to your inner feelings and you will receive the message that the universe is ready to assist you in achieving whatever you desire. *All you have to do is choose to consciously be the love that we are, through loving thoughts, feelings and deeds.*

Tracking Questions

Remember, there are no "right" or "wrong" answers. These questions and exercises are for the purpose of keeping track of your progress. Answer with your first impulse.

1. What does having a "childlike" attitude mean to you?
2. How do you feel about the way you deal with stress?
3. Can you identify three of your transparent beliefs? List them, with a solution for each.
4. What four changes will you make in your thought processes?
5. Are you happy with the way you are experiencing life on a regular basis? List two changes you expect to make, to increase your ability to create solutions instead of excuses for the results you have been experiencing from your attitudes.
6. How does your life style reflect your mental attitude?

Tracking Exercises

Take time to review the process and progress of your journey. A great place to begin is during your moments of meditation and your sleep time. You will be inspired by the wisdom you will be able to extract from your dreams. When you awake, write this information in a journal. Remember to consciously focus your mind on a purpose or intent before you retire.

1. In a state of meditation, live out your dreams.
2. Use your sleeping hours for developing your dream; your subconscious mind will assist you. Keep a dream journal for a week and write down the dreams that are related to your progress.
3. Begin to assimilate the wisdom that will come to you through your experiences. Make a habit of asking yourself each time you come to a crossroad: "What is the moral of

this story?" or: "Why have I created this experience for myself?" Jot down your answers in your journal.

4. Make a list of 20 words you will change from your vocabulary and those words you will substitute for them.

5. Change the following judgmental messages to non-judgmental messages:

   a) When will you ever learn to call me if you are going to be late?

   b) You are mean to pick on your friends all the time.

   c) How can you stand to wear those clothes? Do you think they look good?

   d) I don't know why you are so thoughtless.

Chapter 4

Making Decisions

"People do not lack strength; they lack will."

— Victor Hugo

From our earliest years, making choices is as common to our life as sleeping. A baby decides they want to be in the arms of their mother rather than being held by their mother's friend; I'm sure we have all witnessed this. Teenagers face innumerable decisions: smoking or not, going out instead of doing homework, obeying or disobeying parents' house rules.

Parents too, are constantly faced with challenges: how to potty train a toddler, how to best discipline children, which school child's issues to ignore and which ones to prioritize, deciding whether or not to slow down in a school zone or try to make it through the yellow light—all have implications of choices. Simple matters such as what to prepare for dinner or whether or not to call the doctor when your child has a slight cough, can be challenging decisions.

So how do we come to a decision?

One day, I was sharing concepts of self-worth with one of my special customers. Sitting under a hair dryer, Sally looked up at me and commented, "So it really is all a matter of choices."

"Yes," I replied, sorting through the magazines on the table next to the dryer. "If we have enough information for making wiser choices, instead of relying on others to make those choices for us, we could come to better outcomes. Would you like to read *People's* magazine, *Ladies' Home Journal, New Yorker* or the *Atlantic Monthly?*"

"Do I have to choose?" chuckled Sally. I joined in.

"But—seriously—how do we learn where to get that information necessary for building our decision-making skills?" mused Sally several minutes later when I was finishing up her hair. "Surely our society doesn't teach us to look at the implications or consequences of our choices . . . and then, often it's too late. We have hurt ourselves and others, causing damage that we didn't want . . ."

Looking at Sally in the mirror in front of us, I replied, "Sally, it's easy to rely on old patterns of thinking; it's more difficult to admit we need more knowledge. And it's much more challenging to search it out and come to wiser decisions."

"I feel we have neglected a very important part of our lives by ignoring our own incompetence," she declared.

"Yes," I agreed. "This is why I'm sharing these concepts through the book I'm writing now. I feel there is a moral deficiency in our world today, which I think has to do with the lack of the simple knowledge of how the human brain works."

"What do you mean?"

"If people understood that processes of the human brain are instantly initiated by the selection—conscious or not—of a thought, which in turn electrically triggers the endocrine system to produce chemicals that instantly carry encoded messages to the rest of the human body—to every cell, we would be more careful about making selections—choices about what thoughts we prefer. Because they will, by physiological law, trigger chemical hormones that produce sensations our bodies will experience."

"But how do I stop my thoughts from bringing about old memories?" asked Sally. "For instance: I don't want to continue to feel bad when I pass my husband's grave on my way home every day; I live near the cemetery. It makes me think about him and experience the grief."

"Well, Sally, if you are ready to release that pain, which is initiated by the very sight of the graveyard—for it is a memory that initiates electrical impulses, that in turn trigger the chemical system—you must become conscious of this memory's established path and decide to circumvent it. You must deny the beaten path of mental associations that control you.

"Instead, bring to the forefront those thoughts that cause you to have a different experience. Perhaps you prefer to encounter happiness now."

I put the finishing touches on her hairdo and gave her a hand mirror. As Sally surveyed herself from all angles, she smiled at me in the mirror. Her eyes were shining and there was a lilt in her voice as she declared, "Jeanette, I am definitely through with my old patterns of grief—and those other patterns of guilt, if I don't grieve! I will consciously choose to think about the joy I wish to feel. You always do such a nice job on my hair. It looks great! I feel great! I'm on my way to a New Me!"

The future holds potential for Sally, as it does for every one of us. The past is clouded with intricate neurological connections that have out-served their useful purpose. It is in the present moment—the Now, that we can make choices for personal improvement. Regardless of our age—infant, toddler, teenager or adult—we are faced with choices that will determine what we will experience. Having solid decision-making skills firmly in place makes the selection process easier.

Making Decisions is a Step-by-Step Process

Key # 42 - Sound decisions bring happiness and self-satisfaction; they bring peace of mind and a healthy outlook on life.

In his book, *How to Enjoy Life & Your Job*, Dale Carnegie lists those things most people want:

1. health and the preservation of life
2. food

3. sleep
4. money and the things money will buy
5. life in the hereafter
6. sexual gratification
7. the well-being of our children
8. a feeling of importance

A feeling of importance is the by-product of self-worth. Self-worth is the result of well-developed decision-making skills that you have applied to your daily life.

Remember: Having skills is one thing; to use them in the process of developing your character is yet another. Are you ready to begin?

Key # 43 - When we have sufficient knowledge about the direction we intend to follow, we can proceed with wise choices and enjoy the outcome.

On the other hand, making choices without enough knowledge may result in self-sabotage, loss of confidence and damage to our self-worth. Being in command of your decision-making gives you a simple, clear, straightforward way to deal with choices.

Strong decision-making requires skill, and you will learn how to acquire these skills. They will become the backbone of your life and build your character.

Key # 44 - The power behind that moment in which you make your decision is integrally related to knowing you are accountable for your choices.

Once you have determined where your values lie, you will be motivated to choose options that will bring you close to attaining your goals. Stay focused; know your priorities. Then your decisions will become effortless.

"Action springs out of what we fundamentally desire," wrote Harry A. Overstreet in his illuminating book, *Influencing*

Human Behavior. With drive, focus and determination, you will become the person you most wish to be.

Strength of character consists of three things: 1) trust, 2) power of will, and 3) power of self-restraint. By cultivating sound decision-making skills and strong feelings, you develop firm command over those feelings. You also begin to trust your intuition—the power within, and you start to listen to the messages it delivers.

Check List

Before plunging into any decision, here are three pointers:

1. Freedom of choice and responsibility cannot be separated. If you desire the freedom to decide for yourself, you are solely responsible for that decision.
2. Choices are best made when you are calm. If you are angry, depressed, upset or ill, wait until your mood changes. If you must make an immediate decision, you may wish to allow someone you trust to assist you.
3. Indecision is a decision. It is a decision of no action. Sometimes you may need a period of time before you make a final decision. However, not deciding is a choice you make to refrain from making a decision.

Beware of Apathy

Key # 45 - Know full well if your choices are influenced by others.

Since apathy is the absence of feelings, the apathetic person usually accepts the will of others when making decisions. Often we are not conscious of surrendering our will to others. We don't realize we are letting them be in charge of manifesting our life. When you do not know where your values lie, eventually you manifest problems for yourself. When in doubt, educate yourself about the matter at hand. Education is a tool chest that gives you information you may need in order to make something work for yourself.

Carrie works diligently at improving herself. One day as she sat outside the salon on the bench smoking a cigarette, she launched into a discussion about a matter she was currently dealing with, that had her stymied. "I'm not too sure if I can allow myself to spend the money to go to Europe with my sister," she told me.

I smiled at her and asked, "Have you tried to make a list of your values, and then selected your priorities?"

Making sure she didn't blow the smoke in my direction, Carrie thought for a moment, tamped out her cigarette in the ashtray and asked, "What do you mean?"

"If you take the time to prioritize your values, you will soon be able to make decisions quickly and easily," I explained. "Just try it once; you'll see what I mean!"

Carrie wrote me a postcard from Paris. "THANK YOU SO MUCH, MY FRIEND!!" she printed in bold letters. "I did what you told me! We're having a fabulous time!"

When she returned, she called me. "I made my list of priorities on the very day we talked," said Carrie. "It didn't take me long to realize that it wasn't the money for the trip and not being able to afford it that was the problem. It was my money management and life management in general. I needed to take control of my finances, and track my spending. The trip was a priority, but until I sat down and started to list my values, I didn't have a clear picture of how I could make this trip happen without burdening myself financially. As soon as I focused on making the trip happen, everything else fit in place!"

While she was overseas with her sister, Carrie met a woman from Spain who was interested in selling her hand-made craft items in her boutique.

Seek Role Models

Key # 46 - Surround yourself with successful people whose ideas have led them to achieve their goals.

Use their suggestions, ideas and advice to design your own successful plan. Open your mind and heart to the great thinkers and writers throughout the centuries. Invite them to dine with you as you discuss their works with friends. Spend time reading and re-reading great books. Join a classics book club or invest in a collection of masterpiece writings.

Here is a game I play that I'd like to share with you. It will help you determine where you are with your priorities in life. It also paints a clear picture of your uniqueness:

Take a 3" × 5" index card.

1. On one side at the top, write the name of your favorite animal (you may chose more than one).
2. Under this name, write the numbers 1–4, vertically, or, one number on each line.
3. List after each number, the reasons you prefer that particular animal. These words should be adjectives that describe how you feel about that animal, or how that animal makes you feel, e.g., soft, cuddly, loyal, mysterious, etc.
4. On the other side of the card, write down your favorite color.
5. Again, list four reasons why you selected that color by using four adjectives.

Now—and here is the fun part . . .

6. Carefully look at the adjectives you gave for the animal you selected. These adjectives will tell you what is most important to you in your life—they will deliver your priorities.
7. Turn the card over. These adjectives give you the first and most important clue to what you allow others to see about you—the light in which you want others to see you.

Great! You're off to a great start! Do you know a little more about yourself now?

Other People Influence Your Values

Key # 47 - What you presently value highly has a lot to do with the way you have experienced your relationships with people, places, things and situations in the past.

Everything you saw, heard, smelled, touched, and tasted early in your life has also made an impression on your feelings. For example, if you felt good after your teacher's comments about your watercolor painting of a peacock, at that point, you started to value your artistic talent. When emotions of love surged through your being as you saw a beautiful sunset, at that moment you placed an important value on that experience. Thereafter, you found yourself often enjoying sunsets.

If you felt sad when you heard someone say unkind words to your mother or father, you will harbor unpleasant feelings about that person, or who that person represented to you. You will feel discomfort every time you hear similar words spoken.

If you have been praised for writing well, you will value those related skills. All these impressions are memories which have, at their initial imprint, created neurological associations in your brain. They have become pathways for your electrical impulses. These memories continue to travel the same pathways every time they receive a stimulus that resembles the original impression.

It will be important to become keenly aware of these subtle trigger factors in order to determine if the choices you are making are truly yours, and if they are in alignment with your preferred outcome.

Learn to identify old pathways that you do not wish to continue to travel, and create new ones with your new-found knowledge and focused determination.

Often we think that our choices are made solely by ourselves. However, we may be strongly influenced by five other factors:

1. Past experiences
2. Family
3. Peers
4. Society or the culture in which we live
5. Others (church leaders, coaches, teachers, the bartender, our hairdresser)

The people who belong to these five groups come from varied backgrounds and experiences. They may have a broad spectrum of values. It will be important to allow yourself the right to make your own choices, regardless of others' values or viewpoints. Remember, whatever you choose, you will have to live and experience.

Your Past Experiences Also Influence Your Value System

Tanna shows up about every three months for a haircut; she lives in the mountains of Arizona and owns a stable-cleaning business. One day Tanna arrived with a story about an accident she'd had with her truck. It had slipped in a ravine while pulling a four-horse trailer. She stuck her foot out to brake, causing her to fracture her foot in several places.

Pointing at her foot, Tanna said, "It still hurts once in a while. I feel very awkward and sometimes I'm afraid to drive in them slippery roads in the mountains now." Her face clouded over, "not to mention how awful I felt when I got that big lickin' from my husband when he saw his horse had been hurt."

Her voice quivered. "The guy was more concerned about his horse than about me." I looked at her and nodded; there wasn't anything I could say at that moment. I understood that the truck accident had caused an unforgettable imprint in Tanna's memory. It continues to trigger fear whenever she has to drive the truck and it's raining or snowing and the roads are slippery.

This experience will also conjure up guilt and shame as well as fear, because of her husband's anger and the way he treated her when she returned home. These feelings will influence Tanna's future decisions unless she re-evaluates her thoughts and truly desires to change her outcome in the future.

Another great example of how our past can affect our choices and distort our decision-making skills is the story of Terri and her aunt Cathy. One quiet afternoon I was giving Terri a perm. Terri leafed through a magazine and relaxed while I was worked with her hair.

After several moments of deep thought she turned to me and said, "You know Jeanette, I used to hesitate about getting a perm on my hair."

"Really, and why is that?" I asked.

"Well, when I was little, my Aunt Cathy used to always take me to the beauty shop with her and one time she had her hairdresser give me a perm. What a mistake that was!" she grinned. "My hair got so frizzed that Aunt Cathy had the operator cut it off, as short as possible."

"How did you deal with that?" I asked.

"Man, I felt so ugly, I cried for a whole day!" she chuckled.

"So how did you come to let yourself get a perm again?" I placed a clean white towel on her neck, preparing to proceed with the permanent solution.

"I didn't get a perm again until I was about eighteen. And that was another horrible experience too. The problem that time was that I had bleached my hair and when I got a perm, it fried it!"

I remembered the first time Terri came into the salon to ask about having a permanent. She was hesitant, yet willing to change how her past emotions had affected her. "I'll try it once more." she said, looking in the mirror and describing her new hair style to me.

Her Aunt Cathy's "bad" experiences had caused her to label perms negatively in the past; consequently her decisions were affected by those emotionally charged memories.

Now, with worthy professional advice, she decided to overcome her fears. Terri already knew that the permanent I was giving her would be right for her hair and make her feel even better about herself.

Feeling good about ourselves and the way we look causes us to radiate from within. This inner radiance is translated to the outer world as beauty and explains why beauty is truly in the eyes of the beholder.

Until they realized they were stuck in an emotional pattern that had been established in their past, both Tanna and Terri could not shift gears and change their response from a negative to a positive one. The unwanted feelings associated with similar experiences in the present continued to dictate their choices. "Success" or "failure," "good" or "bad," are only polarity labels given to decisions made from accumulated knowledge.

Past experiences serve as useful reference points, but they need not be the only determining factor for making decisions. The associative and evaluative term "risk" involved in making choices that directly oppose our past experiences often dissolves to become only an "option" when we choose to examine the reasons behind decisions we have made in the past. When we add to this mix a determination to acquire more information from reliable sources that favor a new direction—and then, based on this new information, decide to change our attitudes, feelings and beliefs accordingly—often we discover delightful positive outcomes. The added bonus is feelings of empowerment, self-confidence and self-worth. We have successfully dissolved a myth. It no longer works for us, and thus, we have declared it invalid. What a liberating feeling to be able to break down the barrier of an illusion that had kept us captive!

My friend Ginger used to love horseback riding until the day she had an accident. "Man, when that horse went under the clothes line wires in the back yard, I got thrown off and hit my head so hard on the ground, I swore I'd never get on a horse again!" Ginger declared, as she pulled on her riding boots.

"Are you ready to get on one now?" I asked her.

"I'm certainly going to!" she declared. "I hate to be a slave to my past ... besides I was a kid then. I knew I shouldn't have been riding in the back yard too close to the house. I was only asking for trouble. I'm now ready to be in charge of my life!"

We drove toward the riding stables, laughing at the past. Ginger had clearly focused goals. She loved horseback riding and had decided to dissolve the myth of having future accidents if at all possible, by being more conscious of her actions before starting out.

Know what you are doing, why you are doing it, and where your actions will take you. Make deliberate choices based on this knowledge, information and collected data from past experiences.

Your Family as Influence

Key # 48 - Our behaviors and outcomes are strongly influenced by our decision to imitate or reject our parents' values.

Our first memories are experiences shared with family. Parents, grandparents, siblings and other relatives affect to a great extent the decisions we make.

How were you treated by your family? How did they talk to you? Did they spend time with you? What did you do together? What did they value? How did they view life; what were their outlooks? Attitudes? Were they happy, depressed, frustrated, contrary, tranquil, high-spirited, and determined?

Your Peers as Influence

Key # 49 - The need for peer pressure will disappear as we emerge with our own agendas, our own destinies.

As we grow older, either by chance, parental or personal choice, we create friendships in school, church or temple and the neighborhood where we live. These peers will tend to influence our decisions. At certain times in our lives we want to be different from everyone else. Then we go through a phase when we want to dress, act and talk like our peers. Gangs, sororities, fraternities, secret societies, cults, even religions, are often the outgrowth of this desire to be like everyone else.

At a certain point, moving into adulthood, the motives may become more serious and focused on desired outcomes, such as marrying with a certain social stratum, maintaining blood lines, or property ownership. Some people never outgrow this stage. Their peers will determine their lifestyles and direct their choices thereafter.

However, many of us reach a point in our lives when we want to become butterflies and emerge from the cocoon. We want to make our own choices. At that point, the best equipment we can have will be well-established decision-making skills.

George is a quiet, good-natured man. He was already retired at the time he started coming to my salon every three weeks to get his haircuts. One afternoon, our conversation turned to the past and George started to reflect about his high school days.

"I'll never forget good old Carl. We sure had a lot of fun times together." While I cut his hair, he shared a story about the time he was let down by his peers.

"They had me cornered," he said, his voice quivering with emotion. "I told them I was not going to smoke with them. I soon found out who really were my friends. Carl let me down after he promised to stick by me. Carl had joined the crowd by that time, and there I was, all alone fighting everyone."

Apparently George's decision to stand his ground had cost him his friendship with Carl. It still hurt, obviously, but at that point in his life, George had decided to stand on his own. His peers were not strong enough to break him because by that time he had acquired strong decision-making skills. These allowed him to resist the influence of his peers when their choices went against his well-established values that he believed were best for his own personal destiny.

Your Culture's Society as Influence

Often subliminally or with great subtlety, our culture, heritage and society affect our decision-making process. The media—newspapers, magazines, television, have an effect on our choice-making as well as our value systems. Social, political, economic and religious beliefs, attitudes and issues considered important by our culture often influence our personal decisions as well as our behavior patterns.

Mercedes was a delightful customer who was Mexican by birth.

"I guess I'll always be like my mother, she never had short hair," she remarked as she waited for her son Carlos to have his hair cut.

In Mexican cultural tradition, her role as subservient wife and devoted mother were strong forces that molded her life.

"My husband doesn't want me to wear anything but long hair and dresses," she continued as she gently pushed her black hair off her shoulders.

"I gathered this already," I grinned, as I continued to use the clippers on Carlos.

Mercedes had no desire to break out of the mold. She was happy playing a role that her Mexican culture had created for her. In many ways, it is easy to have someone else tell you what to do and how to act—unless you come to a point in your life when you feel the need to discover who you really are, and "go for the gold"—your ultimate destiny and self-worth as an individual. Conflict only occurs when you are no longer satisfied playing the role. At this point in her life at least, Mercedes is not conflicted.

Key # 50 - Determine if you prefer to experience something different and do so without feelings of guilt.

Sometimes we find ourselves uncomfortable about some of our behaviors which may be reflecting our society's culture. Ask yourself if you wish to follow the influence of your heritage. We have already discussed the destructiveness of guilt. Faster than any other feeling, it devours self-worth, dimming the light within and eventually closing down the path to freedom.

Tall, thin and good-looking, Zac looked like he was from Swedish descent. He had fallen in love with a beautiful Italian girl and they were planning to get married. As I was cutting his hair, he asked: "Do you think I should marry outside of my culture?"

Eying him directly, I responded, "Zac, when you still have questions about a decision you need to make, it only indicates one thing to me: You need more information."

"What do you mean?" He looked at me uneasily.

"If you are still wondering about what direction to go, you do not have enough information, nor are you giving enough energy to the direction you honestly want to take."

Zac winked at himself in the mirror and exclaimed, "You mean I must stop asking myself and others? I must be single-minded toward my heart's desire and enthusiastically pursue it?"

"Yup!" I declared, brushing off his neck and shoulders.

Role models are invaluable. One of my fondest memories is of my 9th grade English teacher, Mrs. LeBaron. She took extra care to help me better understand the English language when I first came to the United States to attend school. Mrs. LeBaron helped me to develop my English diction and writing skills. She was a wonderful role model of a kind and dedicated teacher.

Trish, my neighbor in Reno, NV, told me how the pastor of her church had not only helped her gain more knowledge of the

Scriptures through his stories, but he treated her with caring and understanding. The teachings of the Scriptures now have a profound influence on her life, molding her values and sense of self-worth.

Darvey, a young boy who would always stop by the salon when his mother was there for her hair appointment, used to like to share his stories with me. One day he told me that his coach had been his greatest support as he was growing into manhood. His dad had died before he was old enough to go to school and his coach had encouraged him to participate in sports. He had also encouraged him to be strong when making decisions; to let no one else influence his choices.

This man remained a powerful influence in Darvey's life because he cared about his future, and played a fatherly role in his life. As a result, Darvey has a strong commitment to self-worth and certainty about his values.

Isabel, a beautiful young girl of 22 had fallen in love with Mack, a handsome older man. She had decided to marry Mack. Isabel always was eager to tell me her stories whenever she came to see me at the beauty salon.

Mack, very much in love with his young bride, took her to Texas to live on his ranch. Isabel corresponded with me and in a matter of six months she determined that Mack was not the man she would prefer to live with for the rest of her life. He had become too possessive, hostile and demanding.

Isabel had not gathered enough information about this man, nor had she set her own priorities and established her values before choosing to marry Mack—or any man.

In her letters to me she asked for advice. I advised that she develop a creative and responsible plan for changing her previous decision. She was delighted that I had not only stimulated her creative nature but had also helped her realize that it was okay to change her mind without feeling guilty.

When Isabel shared her revised life plan with Mack, he felt obliged to give her a divorce. He did not take it personally that Isabel was rejecting him; rather, he understood that she was not yet ready for marriage when she had made her decision. "I told Mack I really didn't know who I was or what I wanted, when I accepted his proposal," Isabel wrote. "He understood. After all, he is much older than I, and probably he went through the same experience, making similar mistakes earlier in his life."

Key # 51 - There is a way to redeem yourself and gain strength from a decision you wish to abandon.
You can always make your path take a different turn.

Select What You Value Most

Key # 52 - When you have established strong skills for making decisions, based on knowing your values, the actual process for taking action is easier.

At that point, you cannot allow others or circumstances to dictate your choices. Some decisions are harder to make than others; but when you follow the simple steps outlined here, you will be surprised at how easy it becomes to acquire skills that will serve you well for the rest of your life. Once you acquire proficiency in making decisions, you will avoid the discomforts of "back-tracking."

At first you may not want to seek or accept advice from qualified sources. It only takes a few errors to convince the person who is determined to build character, that listening to others who have earned our respect is often a faster and better way to learn how to avoid pitfalls. Retrieving mistakes uses up valuable energy.

Key # 53 - Before you begin to consider what decision best fits you, first it is important to identify your values.

Having a clear picture in your mind about yourself and your values before you begin to take the steps to making a decision will help make things easier for you.

Make a List of Your Priorities

Make a list of the qualities that are important to you in your life. As you learn to recognize your values, i.e., how you feel about such qualities such as kindness, generosity, tranquility, tolerance and honesty, you form definite opinions. I have listed some examples below.

Which quality do you value above the others? In your journal, make your list in order of priority and add others if they are not included in this list. Referring to the list, you can then make your decisions based on these qualities that you value.

Recognize your feelings toward these qualities as your character. Character is the depth of yourself behind your personality. Your values are your choice, but since your values reflect the experiences you have had with others, you must establish a crystal clear picture of those values. They will determine the direction you will take when making decisions.

Qualities and Character Traits That Form Your Values

- Independent
- Respected by others
- Having good grades in school
- Wealthy, financially
- Having integrity
- Eager to learn and gather knowledge
- Concerned about self-appearance
- Having privacy and honoring others' privacy
- Prompt or on time
- Tenacious
- Honest
- Courteous
- Respect for others' property
- Able to keep secrets

- Healthy
- Articulate
- Appreciative or grateful
- Sincere
- Dependable
- Good listener
- Successful in achieving clearly defined goals
- Focused
- Determined to succeed, against all odds
- Organized

Key # 54 - When facing a decision, make sure you come equipped with your values in order!

This list of values in order of priority will be your instant decision-maker. It will not be difficult to decide if you wish to smoke or not, if optimum health is high on your list of important values.

If your dream is to be successful, it will be easy for you to put marriage and family on hold if you realize you cannot divide your time between the two and can still and still bring about your dream.

For vacation plans, it will be second-nature to choose a quiet mountain cabin over a stay in Las Vegas if you place a high value on quiet, solitude and privacy.

Dianne came to my salon once a month and I had become her sounding board for making decisions. On one of her visits she informed me that her boss had sold the business and now she was being asked to remain with the new owners.

Dianne was not overly attached to her previous boss, but she said if she decided to stay, she would be required to do more work for the same pay as before. Also, her work hours would be changed. This presented a problem since her former work hours coincided with her husband's. The new schedule meant they would have to forfeit some of their time together.

I suggested she make a list of what was important to her in terms of priority. To her surprise, she found her decision simple, once she had sorted out her priorities and was able to see them on paper. She quit her job and immediately found another one that was more interesting, required even less work, and paid more. The hours coincided with her husband's work schedule.

"Wow!" she confessed to me over the phone, "I didn't know it was that easy."

Key # 55 - When necessary, take time to seek counsel from professionals before making your decision.

Sometimes it is not that easy to sort out your priorities and make decisions that complement your values. Situations will arise that will require the help or counsel of others. You may need to collect more information from qualified individuals

Here is a perfect example. Dennis is a young client of mine who had been coming to get his hair cut regularly for about three years. He often talked about his dreaded task of deciding which college to attend after graduating from high school.

"I know I have the power to reason and figure this out myself," he confessed one Friday after school, "but I find it difficult to know where to start."

I shared some simple steps with him and assured him that after he had determined what was important to him he would find it easier to make a wise choice.

This is what I shared with Dennis:

Step # 1 - Identify the situation.   For Dennis it was which college to attend. In his search he found he wanted to be a veterinarian, so his first step would be to find a list of veterinary schools. Some situations can be more complicated than others, but if you simplify them by breaking them down into workable segments they become easier to handle.

For example: If you are choosing a job, you need to know if you prefer working inside in an office, or outdoors; with other people, or alone. Asking yourself these questions gives you a direction to follow and eliminates unwanted conditions. In the process, you eliminate what you least desire.

Make sure you have a clear idea of the problem or challenge. If it seems too large and overwhelming, "chunk it down." Decide what you like best or most. If you've had experiences that already have given you clues, apply this knowledge to the challenge at hand.

Step # 2 - Write down all possible alternatives. Dennis was considering an out-of-town college but when he started to write down the costs, his decision was easily made. He would begin his general education program in a junior college nearby. Writing things down is important because it helps to have a visual concept of things. Once you become more proficient you can do this step mentally.

Consider every possibility you can think of. You will come to recognize why these options will not be the selected ones, and down the road, this will be another serviceable skill for you. Next time you will not have a problem deciding for or against an action.

Step # 3 - Gather information about the specific situation. For Dennis this step was exciting. He found himself visiting new places to gather information, such as the Chamber of Commerce, libraries, several junior colleges in the area, colleges of veterinary medicine and a number of different veterinary hospitals.

He also spent a great deal of time on the Internet. Dennis discovered that having the facts before he made his decision saved him considerable frustration, time and energy.

In addition, Dennis interviewed many professionals in the field of veterinary medicine. This database of knowledge will continue to be valuable as he pursues his career and eventually establishes himself professionally. He will add to it and keep it up to date. It will become one of his most valuable resources

Step # 4 - Consider the consequences. When Dennis began the process of financial planning he found it easier to come to a decision after he was able to see his figures on paper. As you look at your possible options, it is necessary also to consider the alternatives by carefully looking at the conflicting as well as the constructive consequences.

A simple and fun way to do this is to ask yourself, "What could possibly be the worst scenario?" Placing yourself in that situation or circumstance will help you recognize reasons why you will not choose that option.

This reinforces your skills, because down the line your strong invalidating response will have made a vivid impression on your senses. Weak decisions in your past brought about nullifying outcomes. By using these as points of reference, now you are able to make choices you can live with more comfortably.

Selecting a new direction sometimes means removing yourself from situations and friendships you may have valued before. As you grow in strength, trusting your intuition, you come to discover new windows for growth. The important thing to remember here is that these seemingly difficult decisions are a normal process of developing your unique character. This requires unshakable personal responsibility.

Step # 5 - Make a choice. As Dennis came to this step, he was already having too much fun. This is the attitude that helps us arrive at healthier decisions. The best way to execute this step is to sit quietly, gather all your internal strength, meditate, avoid contrary emotions and listen to your inner force. Then allow yourself to be completely immersed in the feeling of being already in the midst of this choice. For example, Dennis would see himself as a veterinarian already practicing his profession. This is the game of "what if" that allows us to project ourselves into the future, stay focused, and determined to succeed, regardless of the odds.

Make sure your selection fits appropriately with your values. Even though Dennis thought he wanted to become a veterinarian and he had conducted extensive research already, still, I insisted that he ask himself, "Is this really the outcome I want for myself, my life?"

Make this step a quick one. The sooner you make a decision after you have your list of the most possible selections, the faster you will feel the relief that is empirical to decision making. It will be a weight off your mind. This decision must align with your most important values, or you have solved nothing.

Step # 6 - Take action with dignity. I reminded Dennis that taking action sometimes involves risking the unknown; but the unknown is where you must go if you are going to evolve into a person of great self-worth and happiness beyond your dreams. Taking risks is a normal part of growing, learning and establishing what is most important to you. Eliminate fears that only destroy your courage.

Once you have taken all of these six steps, you will be more knowledgeable and less likely to make ignorant decisions with harmful outcomes. But there is still one more important step, after you have taken action.

Step # 7 - Follow-up. There was one more thing I had to share with Dennis. I asked him before he left one afternoon after his monthly haircut, "Suppose, after having made a decision, you find yourself not liking the consequences of your choice? What then?"

"Hmm," he shook his head ruefully. "I never thought about that."

I smiled and placed a hand on his shoulder. "Evaluate how your choice complements your unique style. Making the best of a decision does not mean you have no alternatives and must stick to your initial decision. If the original decision does not feel comfortable to you, it is a sign that something must be reconsidered.

"Your feelings of comfort or discomfort are clues about your inner make-up and your sincere dreams. Give yourself enough time, as long as 21 days, to determine if the feelings of discomfort are related to the fact that you are about to embark on a change in your life—or to having made a decision to do something you really don't want to do.

"Go within often, at least three times a day, to check your feelings and find the origin of your discomfort."

Dennis was eager to make sure he was on the right track. "How will I know when I'm there?"

"Ask yourself: Can I live with this choice happily? If not, go back and follow steps #1 through #6 again," I advised.

He grinned broadly and exclaimed, "I'll never be able to thank you enough for what I've learned as I was getting my haircuts from you all this time!"

I was honored by his gratitude. "You're very welcome, Dennis!" We both felt a special bonding. I knew my method was working for him.

Key # 56 - If you made a decision that produced undesirable or unwanted consequences, don't let this single experience destroy your life forever!

The experience will serve as a tool or point of reference for your growth and enlightenment. You can always figure out a responsible and creative way to make the best of the original decision and then proceed with more caution the next time.

Also, if you feel unhappy with the result of any decision you made, remember, nothing has to be permanent. You can always make another decision. You must not feel like a failure for having to change your mind.

"We're afraid of change," says Leo Buscaglia, Ph.D. in his book, *Living, Loving and Learning*. You may not make the best decision the first time. As with anything in life, practicing skills makes for greater performances!

"Never forget this," I had said to Dennis on one of his trips in to see me, "you always have a choice. You can always change your decision, but don't feel guilty about it!"

I insisted that he know one thing: "Always forgive yourself." After all, you have a right to feel wonderful about your decisions. Evaluation is an effective, normal and natural process of enjoying your self-worth. Discovering new ways of doing things adds to your skills and allows you to point out things you will not repeat.

You can be proud of yourself when your choices have successful outcomes; just don't be afraid of change. Remember: "That which you fear shall come upon you."

Don't be Discouraged

Key # 57 - Don't allow discouragement to deplete your precious energy.

If previous choices have brought unsatisfactory results, we can become discouraged and stressed. Many times guilt sets in. Perhaps we will proceed with too much caution the next time. These are normal, healthy responses; but their consequences on the body and mind can be unhealthy, if we don't recognize them for what they are and nip them in the bud.

Conflicting Decisions

You may find yourself in situations in which two important values conflict. For example: As a youngster you may have been asked by a friend to go to a party where the guests were expected to drink, take drugs or have sex with multiple partners. You knew your parents did not approve of these activities, and you also knew their disapproval was based on consequences: getting caught and ending up in jail, ruining your future opportunities by having a mark on your record, ending up with a sexually transmitted disease, getting into a car accident and being charged for DUI, etc.

You valued honesty and you also valued your friendship with the person who invited you. You had to determine what was most important to you: the friendship or honesty. You had to use sharp, well-developed skills in making your decision.

If you had already made honesty a priority high on your list, the decision would be a snap. If your friend held values different from those of your parents, and if you valued your parents' concern for your welfare and were well versed yourself about the consequences of attending the party, the decision would also be a snap.

Key # 58 - Once you have become comfortable with what is most important to you, decisions come quickly.

When you have acquired the skills for making sound choices, it will be easy to decide anything.

Challenges are Stepping-Stones to Success

We admire the challenges that deliver well-polished skills. Witness the excitement and verve of a tennis or baseball player, dancer or pianist when ready for a game or performance.

If you take a look at your body's ability to serve you in all aspects of your life, you will discover how the hormones assist you in your tasks. Adrenalin kicks in when you are excited.

Endorphins flow when you experience happiness; your pupils enlarge when you look at something beautiful.

Key # 59 - Making our own choices is a natural and enriching ability when we are prepared to use our innateness.

Discovering creative ways to make and act on decisions puts you in control of your destiny. You feel successful because you are the only one who is responsible for your life. No one is pulling your strings or making you do something against your will.

Transformation Signs

Key # 60 - Your signs of transformation will include your ability to have a more positive outlook.

Once you have established a pattern of making decisions without hesitation, you will soon sense your alertness. You will have a more flexible, open-minded attitude and a sharpened ability to remember things that help in making decisions with ease.

You will also be surprised to discover that once you become more effective in making decisions, you will sharpen your capacity to initiate new and creative activities. All of your values are important, but when you know which ones are of most importance to you, making decisions becomes easier and more fun.

The fun of making decisions is one of the factors most commonly overlooked. You will look forward to this process without fearing the issues involved and without dreading the outcome.

Others will discover that you have become more optimistic about the past, present and future.

Tracking Questions

Here we are again at the end of another chapter. Time to polish your skills. Journal and pencil ready?

1. Would you be able to easily resist the pressure of deciding against your values from someone who is your friend today?
2. Who are some of the people you feel have influenced your choices?
3. What 5 concepts have you followed in making choices before reading this book?
4. How would you describe your feelings when you have made a wise choice?
5. Have you punished yourself in the past for not making a wise choice?
6. Have you been able to identify your values? Why? Why not?

Tracking Exercises

1. Write down a few words or a short statement about a decision you need to make now.
2. Write your options as they come to you.
3. Focus on each option quietly and unemotionally. Use meditation techniques if you wish.
4. Ask when considering each option: "Where will this choice take me?" See yourself at the end of each mentally chosen road.
5. Pay close attention to how you feel when considering each option. Write down these feelings in your journal.
6. Select the option that gives you the greatest feeling of peace. Describe this feeling in your journal.

Chapter 5

Establishing Quality in Life

"I'm an artist at living, and my work of art is my life."

— Suzuki, a Zen Master

Evaluate your progress. Measure each step forward by asking simple questions:

- Do I like the consequences of my actions based on the decisions I have made?
- Am I happier?
- How does this new choice make me feel?
- Has my life improved? How? List the ways your life has improved.
- What else has changed in my life as a result of these new decisions?
- What do I still need to do in order to reach my goals or accomplish what I have set out to do?
- Can I detect new challenges that have arisen that are a result of decisions, choices, or actions I have taken?
- Am I heading toward my goal, i.e., a quality life for myself?

Key # 61 - Monitoring your changes is one of the most valuable aspects of your journey.

Monitoring not only makes progress and success a visible experience; it also makes it easier to change your course of action immediately, rather than having to backtrack later on—and pay the consequences of lost time, energy and possibly money.

You will know when you are on the right track because you will feel it. It is a special, indescribable "sense" or resonance. You will also be able to witness improvements as your charted journey unfolds. They will appear right before your eyes, like a magical picture when touched by an enchanted stylus.

You have come this far, but perhaps you're still not sure what you and others mean by a *quality life*. Surely before you continue, this definition should be clear in your mind. Before we can achieve our dreams in life, we have to be able to clearly define every term that is associated with those dreams.

Somewhere I ran across a little story that goes something like this:

"Your task," God said, "is to build a better world."

"But how?" I asked. "This world is so vast and complex, and I am so small and insignificant. There is nothing much I can do. Look at all the power struggles that are going on—and have always gone on. I am not at the helm. I don't have the power, money, influence ..."

"No one is asking you to do anything more than just build a better you." God replied. "That's all anyone can ever ask!"

I knew there was great wisdom in these words, just as I knew there was a catch. The words were telling me I didn't have to be an activist and wave flags or march in parades. Instead, they were instructing me to do something far more challenging.

At that moment I realized more than ever, that "it all begins with me."

Key # 62 - Commitment and dedication to personal improvement are part of developing our character and establishing a strong and firm foundation for excellence in life.

My dream would be to set an example not for others, but for myself. In the process, if others "caught on," so much the better. Like the Hundredth Monkey Principle, as soon as there is a critical mass that is manifesting and experiencing a quality life, by the natural law of mathematics, the world will start to become a better place for everyone.

This sounded so idealistic I felt like a Pollyanna, but I also knew it was a reachable dream. It was something I could get my arms around. And after all, wasn't it enough to ask of anyone, to control their own destiny and create a quality life just for themselves? Wasn't it enough just for me to strive for excellence? I already knew from past experience that biting off more than I could chew left me feeling frustrated, overwhelmed and ultimately depressed and defeated.

Key # 63 - "Quality" refers to choices you or others have made that are based on a set of values.

These values represent excellence. Perhaps you have seen "quality meat" or "choice beef" labels in the supermarket. Inspectors have placed their stamp of excellence on the meat after examining it according to certain established values.

You create a quality life for yourself after you have made your list of values (Chapter 4) and given them an order of priority. You are now making decisions in your life, based on this priority list of values, and the dreams you intend to dream.

You are also focusing on those dreams and putting your innate powers to work by deliberately creating what you prefer to experience. You are *consciously* making sure you track your thoughts, feelings and words in order to eliminate denial of unwanted or transparent beliefs. You are visualizing your outcomes and practicing "as if"—seeing yourself as already having achieved your dreams.

And finally, you are acknowledging the spark of light within. You are driving your vehicle with universal principles at your side. You are practicing certain natural laws of the cosmos:

1. The Golden Rule of doing for others as you would do for yourself.
2. Compassion for others.
3. Interaction with others, without judgment or regret.
4. Forgiveness for yourself and others.
5. Gratitude for the experiences that result from our choices, decisions and actions; whether the outcome appears to be "good" or "bad," knowing these are only polarity judgment words, perceptions based on our current state of affairs. Tomorrow we may see the value in an experience that today may seem painful, shameful, fearsome, damaging, etc.

Key # 64 - Practice leads to improvement!

Like other skills, these virtues may take time to develop. Be patient with yourself. The cultivation of anything of value requires attention (consciousness) and gestation (time) before it reaches fruition (fulfillment).

Key # 65 - Experiences involve relationships with others, yourself or nature.

They create a drama or story of interaction. Remember that each of us is a spark of divinity creating a reality for ourselves. You can view the same issue from many sides. Someone once said, "We all get to be on the soap box." How true that is!

Also, be willing and ready to ask yourself: "Is this my creation or is it 'their' creation in which I am choosing to become involved?" Determine if you are indeed deliberately creating what you choose to experience. Stay in the driver's seat of your own destiny.

Remember: You experience deliberately what you create intentionally. Review your list of values and the priority you have given them. Whenever necessary, review and revise your list of dreams—what you prefer to experience.

Key # 66 - Life created intentionally implies a will to be involved in the adventure.

Abstinence is a self-imposed imprisonment that leads to stress: frustration, restlessness, fear, depression, and a host of other unwanted habits and behaviors. Pursue excellence and a quality life with a passion! Exciting, rewarding, nourishing experiences and adventures will follow.

Once you have established quality in your life you will find that you no longer have physical or emotional exhaustion. These symptoms indicate you are playing a role that doesn't resonate with your list of values or your dreams. This pressure causes anxiety, inaction and stagnation.

In a weakened depleted state you will tend to merely repeat past mistakes because you are locked into someone else's plans for you. You will be imitating or modeling behaviors, habits and a lifestyle that are not "you" and do not represent your wishes and desires. At any point along the way, if you sense this starting to happen to you—and you will, if you are conscientiously tracking your self-worth—stop! Take notice. Check out your lists. Monitor your feelings. Make new choices. Decide to take action in order to bring yourself back on track with your values and dreams.

And then, act on your decision.

Key # 67 - Wisdom comes as a result of having taken the risk into the unknown to recover the truth of your being.

Stress and anxiety may be included in the baggage of emotions you will find yourself carrying ... but no one is asking you to shoulder this load of empty (invalidating) or worthless cargo. Let go!

Weather changes minute by minute. You can change just as quickly. You do not have to linger in any emotional storm too long. Stay focused; keep your intentions foremost in your mind at all times. This mind set will easily dissipate any storm clouds on the horizon.

Harmony and Balance—The Rewards of Risk-taking

Key # 68 - Harmony is the twin sibling of balance.

Once you experience the tracking process, you will know how gratifying it feels to have your life return to its natural state of balance. Your life will hum and you will feel happy inside, even if the whole world around you seems to be falling apart . . . even if others are in a state of despair.

Does it seem unfair or selfish for you to feel so fulfilled? Not at all. You are now taking a leadership role. You are setting an example for others.

In the Scriptures it says, "If I am not for myself, who will be for me?" Remember, The Source is within you in that powerful vehicle you are driving!

Others will comment on your renewed sense of self-confidence, which in turn brings a greater desire to live a richer life. You will find new reserves of energy for the delightful small and meaningful aspects of life: a day of sunshine, a beautiful new bud on your rose plant, a butterfly in the garden, the laughter of a baby in the supermarket, the response you receive from a "thank you" at the service station.

You will have increased desire to participate in vibrant relationships and be experiencing a greater sense of joy and happiness. Happiness emerges from the environment we create for ourselves. Joy comes from within. Joy is a quiet inner state of being.

As you become more conscious of your choices and base these choices on your value system as well as your standards of excellence, you will create a quality life. Your complaining, grumbling and weeping will be a thing of the past.

Victor, the Quality Man

Once there was a sweet elderly man who lived in an extremely modest home in the outskirts of a large village. This old man consciously created what was valuable to him.

Victor spent much of his time at the village's senior center; everyone at the center inevitably congregated around him as if he were selling snake oil on the street corner. I became interested in Victor when I was doing research on geriatrics for my Sociology class in college. He became the focus of my paper because he was exemplary for his quality of life.

Victor began his day by greeting everyone with a cheerful word and a friendly smile.

"It takes 72 muscles to frown, only 14 to smile," he said to me as he pulled up a chair for me to sit by him in the conference room. Victor never had too much to explain; he simply stated facts. But he knew how to tell a story with a moral, and deliver the point of the story with the clarity of a full moon on a summer night.

He always remembered everyone's name. "The sweetest music to most people's ears is the sound of their own name, Jeanette," he declared, giving me a warm smile as he looked straight into my eyes.

"If you want to have a friend, be a friend," came the quick reply after I interviewed him one day in the garden. "Speak and act as if everything you do is a genuine pleasure," he added, handing me a beautiful rose he had picked as we strolled down the well-kept path.

Victor was genuinely interested in people. "You can like almost everybody if you try," he said with a twinkle in his eye.

I interviewed Victor's friends and they said Victor was always generous with praise. They felt he had been cautious with criticism if it ever was needed during their little circle meetings.

I observed that Victor was considerate about the feelings of others. "There are usually three sides to a controversy," he said to me as I was writing down some of his gems of wisdom in my notes. "Yours, the other's, and the right side." In his years, he had acquired a serenity about himself, one which was enjoyed by those who listened to his tales.

"What counts most in life," I heard him say to Vera, the receptionist, "is what we do for others." He turned to me and winked. Victor had a fabulous sense of humor, dry but subtle and creative.

Victor never lacked patience. If you ever found him sitting quietly facing the big picture window in the foyer of the senior center, you would feel and possibly even see an aura of humility about him. Victor rewarded my visits many times over by simply being himself, smiling and listening to others tell of their lives. I walked away from that senior center with a gift of life to share with the world.

Everyone Is Different

Key # 69 - To add quality to your life, you will be learning about people, places and cultures.

You will have realized by now that education is an ongoing process. It includes receiving degrees and certificates from accredited academic and vocational institutions; traveling; reading; participating in seminars, workshops, distance learning and other internet educational offerings; surfing the Net; watching educational cable TV.

Education also includes our daily encounters with people, places, circumstances and conditions. Ultimately, education will give you a basis or foundation for being comfortable with everyone, regardless of their creed, color or status in life. You will also have acquired the tools to be able to learn from everyone you meet.

My mother, like Victor, was an example of a broadly educated person. She was just as comfortable and lovely in the presence of those who lived in material wealth as in the presence of people of humble means. She had a delicate manner about her that blended well in all cultures. Born and raised in the land of the Mayas, she spent her days traveling to their many colorful villages in the beautiful country of Guatemala. She taught the precepts of a quality life and helped many to understand the value of self-fulfillment and self-worth.

"Each of us uses different and unique methods of learning about life and ourselves," I often heard my mother say. "Each method will bear the same fruits that teach about the discovery of value."

I remember her wise advice one sunny afternoon many years ago, as we took a leisurely ride on the boat around the enchanted Lake Atitlan. "An attitude of love for others, by understanding first ourselves, categorically surfaces like an underwater diver when reaching for fresh air," she told me. Somehow, she always managed to be inconspicuous in her own method of teaching others, much like my "Papito," her father.

In his book, *The Way of Life According to Laotzu*, Bynner writes, "A leader is best when people barely know that he exists, not so good when people obey and acclaim him, worst when they despise him ... But a good leader, who talks little, when his work is done, his aim fulfilled, they will all say, 'We did this ourselves.'" This aptly describes my mother's method of teaching.

Independence Engenders Trust

Key # 70 - When we refrain from meddling with people, they seem to take care of themselves.

I applied this philosophy as a parent of my seven children. I found that when I did not issue commands, they behaved better. I also did not preach to them. As adults, all of my children have established a certain quality of life appropriate to their individual and unique expression. Their experiences have brought them to recognize their own values for a quality life and to express themselves as happy individuals.

I didn't impose any "rules" on them. Instead, I taught them how to create their own guidelines, based on the perceived and understood consequences of their actions. Thus, they learned how to take responsibility for their lives.

Each child has thanked me for having shared with them my wisdom (knowledge plus experience) throughout their lives as a friend and not a doting parent.

I listened to them and when necessary, I asked for their explanations in order to be able to understand a joke, or a specific (complex) teenager's behavior. This engendered a trust and love among us, creating a unit of caring, self-respecting individuals.

Pessimism Must Be Reversed

Key # 71 - Life is a process; journeying toward our dreams is a process.

Feelings of dissatisfaction and failure run down the morale of any person or society. Reaching a desired dream is only part of a journey. Indeed, getting caught up in the pursuit of the dream often causes us to lose sight of the valuable present moment. This may lead to feelings of failure that in turn can attack that powerful inner spark and destroy our drive and enthusiasm for life.

Becoming more process-oriented allows us to appreciate the scenery along the way; to seize the moment and "live in the Now." We can overcome helplessness and pessimism by starting to trust the process, and trust ourselves.

Pay attention to intention; we talked about this before (Chapter 3). Our intentions are ignited by the intensity of our own feelings of self-worth. Focus on respect for your values and your dreams. Visualize yourself as the achiever, the successful person who has all the qualities you most admire. Build your character on that visualization. Select role models or other individuals who possess those qualities you admire most. Self-imaging and focused attention on your intention will create a strong fortress against pessimism and feelings of helplessness.

Dare To Be Different

Key # 72 - Quality of life does not mean equality.

Each of us has a special and personal gift to share with others. It is the recognition of our uniqueness and our special gifts that bonds us together in appreciation and gratitude. We come into this world with a freshness, a new way of expressing ourselves to others.

We are also uniquely involved with our own world. However, our uniqueness needn't be an excuse for refraining to contribute our "design" with its special signature.

Have you ever witnessed the distress of a teenager? Much of this is caused by their strong attempts to imitate each other. Some teenagers spend much of their time mimicking their idols or the role models they have chosen. In the process, their creativity diminishes, their self-worth is capsized by others and their success floats away down the river.

We become our own demons of destruction when we determine to follow the fads and fashions. In the process we destroy our innate creative ability as well as our uniqueness. Teenagers as well as adults who are afraid to acknowledge their authentic selves can easily be seduced by clever marketing schemes that cater to their vulnerability.

Quality of life comes from deliberately creating our own reality through the greatest channel there is—ourselves! You may have heard the statement: "I have to find myself before I can be myself." My suggestion to those who are searching is to go within, and listen and love what you find.

Competition Can Be a Friend, Not a Foe

Key # 73 - Competition can destroy the pure intent of any event.

However, competition needn't be a culprit. You can turn it around to become a doorway to expressing your uniqueness.

My friend Joyce owned a used bookstore where she creatively displayed her wares. She began to feel other bookstores around town were interfering with her business, resulting in less traffic to her store. Because she was afraid of losing all of her customers and being forced to close down the store, she decided to take in a partner.

Encouraged by her partner, Joyce became more competitive, overlooking her true intent and creating a monster for herself. Business became a battlefield of bitterness and hostility that ultimately destroyed the delightful environment of the store with its unique qualities of warmth and intimacy.

In contrast, I will share the decisions I made in my business when I was faced with comments from others that beauty salons were a dime a dozen in our town. With inspiration from my father, who was always eager to share his secrets as a wise businessman, I was secure enough to know that the number of salons could not be a threat to my business.

Daddy always told me that it was the quality of my business that mattered, and this aspect would continue to attract clientele. I knew that quality work, a positive attitude and excellent customer service are the factors that determine the outcome of a successful business venture.

I had spent years developing my talents as a hair dresser and designer, and I had learned and applied much wisdom from both of my parents, about human relationships and business practices. Thus, competition was not a threat, since it didn't take long for those who were looking for quality work to find it within the doors of my beauty salon.

The love and passion for one's work, teamed with applied wisdom, create the foundation for the desired outcome.

Key # 74 - Excellence comes as a gift when specializing in your field of endeavor.

Competition exists in any endeavor, but it does not have to be the motivating factor to success. Motives that begin with competitive win/lose relationships and the intention to destroy a perceived enemy, end up destroying the passion that engendered the desire to create. Winning becomes a game of destruction and the result is failure.

My friend Kay had a keen sense for the art of flower arranging. She bought a flower shop and dedicated the next two years to the development of her business with great success. Her secret: "I offered 'specialty items' which made every customer feel important and delighted with the service I provide." She divulged this to me one day as she delivered the weekly complimentary bouquet for display in my shop.

Her passion for her art continued to reward her with delightful returns. "When you love what you do, you get good at it," said Kay as she scooted out the door. And in the process, everyone wins.

Create the Masterpiece—Wake Up Your Senses

Key # 75 - Experiencing the senses and responding to them awakens your passion for life.

Our senses make us feel truly alive. They add an orchid to the quality bouquet of our life.

One way to initiate a quality life is to focus on creating a passion for your dreams. Develop your senses: touch, taste, seeing, hearing and smelling. The smell of scented candles ... a burning campfire ... the first blossoms of spring ... the sight of a snow-capped mountain ... the desert blooming in spring ... tall ocean waves ... the soft furriness of a new-born kitten ... the sharp prickle of a rose thorn ... the pungent taste of special wine ... the succulence of a fresh orange ... the sound of thunder when it storms ... the echo of your voice as you shout across the valley ... the exquisite sound of the violin performing a Bach "Partita" ... the sounds of creatures in the forest ... the sound of rain on a cabin rooftop....

Passion, deep appreciation ignites the spirit and delivers a powerful surge of energy and profound sense of joy that you can intentionally direct toward your life purpose or destiny.

Get excited about your dreams. Express your enthusiasm to others. Spread the good energy!

Wisdom Comes through Experience

Key # 76 - The circumstances and relationships you encounter reward you with knowledge about yourself.

Whether you perceive these experiences as "good" or "bad," they have a definite purpose that is integrally related to the development of your self-worth. Knowledge plus experience equals wisdom, the fruit from the blossom that makes us more aware and receptive, adding quality to our life. Once we grasp a full understanding of self-empowerment and start to own our experiences, we realize that we are the subject, not the object of our experiences. They do not happen to us; we happen to create them—for a reason.

They don't just happen; they happen just.

We learn to ask questions such as: "Why did I create this?" "What is the purpose for this experience?" and "What am I to extract from this?"

As we go within for answers, we learn to respect and trust our intuition, that inner voice. As you make a habit of going with your hunches and getting favorable results, you will begin to sense a feeling of inner harmony. This feeling is a strong building block for developing character and self-worth.

The success of your life's experiences depend on whether or not you want to own them.

Becoming your own best observer will soon be second-nature. You will discover that it leads to a more practical attitude and outlook because you will place a beneficial value on every experience; recognizing that you bring them to yourself for an important reason.

What Is the Moral of Your Story?

Soon you will be able to extract the moral from the story of your life that you are writing—and living. When you can do this with ease, you will embark on the next chapter or event without "baggage." "What did I learn from this?" will deliver the reason for the experience and put it into perspective with your dreams. With great enthusiasm, gratitude and self-forgiveness, if necessary, you will close that chapter and eagerly await the next one.

Key # 77 - The passion-filled thrust we give to every involvement is the deliberate and intentional living of our dream.

The changes we will be making bring growth and new life. Anything new, different or untried may seem strange and fearful. Don't allow fear to hamper or destroy the progress of your full expression.

When you are happy, others will notice. When they feel your radiance and well-being, they will also become happier—for you, and for themselves. Smiles are contagious. Keep expressing the true self you are discovering, and continue to believe in yourself … It's that simple!

Key # 78 - If you experience doubt at any time, recall your successes.

Re-trace the steps leading to your successes. Re-discover the feeling of trust in yourself. If you have a desire to gain a promotion, for example, but have surrendered to a doubting mind, create the dream again. If you wish to obtain respect from your children, consider it done, and then take the next step in faith and expectancy.

Perhaps a yacht in the Bahamas or a house in Ireland is your dream come true; release the fear of lack, loss or limitation and see yourself already cruising in your yacht, exploring the islands, meeting new people, walking the streets of Dublin, planting your flower garden … Maybe you want to stop smoking or lose some weight. Take yourself to the finished step and celebrate your success. Perhaps your dream is to better understand your spouse or your parents; or maybe you wish to be more pleasant to your associates. I'll never forget my client and good friend Julie's suggestion: "Fake it till you make it; before you know it, you'll be there."

Galileo was known to have said: "You cannot teach a man anything; you can only help him find it within himself." This is great wisdom. The spark within you will ignite your life—if you want it to. When you need answers, you will know to go within to find them.

Be Still—Notice What You Tell Yourself

How do you sense or understand the language you are hearing and feeling when you go within? Sometimes our busy, often hectic life seems to lack a focal point. Too often we take short cuts by looking for fast solutions or answers to our questions. These "quick fixes" may keep us from affirming the truth within.

Key # 79 - The best way to understand the language of your inner self is to start paying attention to messages from your physical body.

Since the body and mind are integrally connected and cannot be separated, by nature, a good communication system with your body will lead to understanding your mind. This focused interactive relationship will soon allow you to access your spiritual self at will.

Let's start with the physical body. You may enjoy a daily exercise routine. Or you may be one of those energetic individuals who regularly hikes up a mountain road or takes long bike rides. Some of you may prefer to explore and test new diet programs. Perhaps you take vitamins and herbal supplements, or work out at a gym. You may have your own fitness trainer coming to your home to design your personal health program. Still others may simply do nothing at all except "keep on keeping on," hoping that one day they can swallow a magic pill that will deliver the clear mind and perfect body shape they would like to have.

In truth, paying attention to your physical body's messages does not necessarily relate to any of these regimens or schemes. Keeping physically fit first requires a keen mind, and taking time to listen to your inner wisdom. All else will follow.

Think of Yourself as a Mind

Think of yourself as a mind, for in reality, this is what you are. You do not have a mind. You are Mind! You have a "brain" where consciousness and subconsciousness reside. Your conscious mind is your personality, the accumulation of all neural-net connections from this life time—the neo-cortex. Your subconscious mind is where your "Self" resides—the cerebellum. The conscious mind reasons, judges and demands explanations. Your subconscious is where the "all knowing intelligence"—the collective consciousness silently resides, until you "ask" for its wisdom to come forth.

A psychological fact: The subconscious creates according to programming—the wisdom of all ages.

A metaphysical fact: The activities of the subconscious are fundamentally constructive, for it operates under the direct influence of Cosmic Consciousness.

In order to re-program our lives, we need to silence the conscious mind in order to access from the subconscious mind the answers we desire! How do we do this?

Key # 80 - The process of meditation is one of the oldest and most effective ways to access guidance from our subconscious mind, and thus re-program our thought process.

The mind is powerful and infinitely creative. Remember that! You have established an Ideal Self in your mind. This is the You that you are striving to become the "essential" you. You are well aware that you have not yet achieved this Ideal Self, so it will not help—in fact, it may hinder—to compare this ideal to the person you are, right now. It may cause you to see your-self as a failure; and what you see, you will become ... thus, destroying your "dream" or ideal.

Be Still and Listen

Key # 81 - When you "go within," you will find the real power behind the entire process of manifesting your self-worth and a quality life.

Think of yourself as a spiritual being that took on a body-mind consciousness for creating earthly dreams out of spiritual visions.

Ask your own light within—your subconscious mind, to guide you. Become more aware of your own message codes; listen and then listen some more. Spend time journaling so you can see a pattern of your own responses to your questions. Be still, very still before you act! Acting will come soon enough. Pay attention and value that still small voice within. This will strengthen your ability to follow your intuitive feelings. Become the "silent observer."

Eventually you will become so familiar with your feelings, you will be able to determine the separate meanings they have for you. The more you practice this technique of listening and going within, the easier it will become. It is like learning a new language.

Focused Attention Brings Results

Before you sit down to meditate, ask yourself: "Am I focused enough on my daily life to begin my meditation?"

Key # 82 - The art of being conscious—concentrating and paying attention—begins in daily life.

We usually have trouble concentrating for one simple reason: we are usually not consciously present as we move through life. Most of the time we cannot concentrate because we don't really see what we are looking at; nor do we listen to what we are hearing. Too often we get lost in the plans for the day, a problem at work, what we're going to cook for dinner, and so on. In other words, we usually live in the future and the past, not in the present.

Eighty-five-year-old Clara, one of my wise clients, once said to me, "The past is gone, the future never comes. But The Now is your gift. That is why we call it the 'present.'" Clara became one of my teachers.

Practice the process of feeling a connection with every energy that emanates in the world around you. In this state of mind you will find you can enter into a meditative state with greater power of concentration. It is "contemplation" that allows the meditative process to occur.

To create the foundation for a quality life, I discovered four steps for initiating new ideas:

1. *Establish the Groundwork*: Investigate the situation actively.
2. *Incubation*: Do not think about the situation actively; let the subconscious take over.
3. *Enlightenment*: "Out of the blue," some idea will suggest itself.
4. *Confirmation*: Consciously consider that idea. Details and aspects associated with the situation will elaborate on your insight.

The Art of Meditation

The Director of the new Laboratory for Brain Imaging and Behavior at University of Wisconsin-Madison in conjunction with other scientists, asked the Dalai Lama to provide information concerning his approach to meditation. These scientists strongly believe that meditation practices are beneficial to mental and physical health. Buddhists monks have known for centuries that meditation can alter the mind. Now, through technology, scientists are studying changes that occur to the brain during the process of meditation, and the exact location of those changes.

It is written in the Dead Sea Scrolls: "I have reached the inner vision and through Thy spirit in me I have heard Thy wondrous secret. Through Thy mystic insight Thou hast caused a spring of knowledge to well up within me, a fountain of power, pouring forth living waters, a flood of love and of all-embracing wisdom like the splendor of eternal light."

J. Krishnamurti writes: "A meditative mind is silent. It is not the silence of a still evening. It is the silence when thought with all its images, its work, and its perceptions has entirely ceased."

Key # 83 - Entering this sacred silence through meditation is the beginning of being able to communicate with the Self—the subconscious mind.

You might be surprised to know that meditation is as natural as breathing. Experiencing the silence of the mind is actually an easy process. I know you talk to yourself, but have you ever listened to your inner wisdom? Rediscovering the techniques that move us into stillness is an adventure any explorer will enjoy.

When outside pressures begin to take a toll on me and disrupt my personal harmony, I start to feel tense. The first thing I do is tell myself to relax. Then I close my eyes and go within, to seek a silent moment. Once within, I focus on divine light and love.

Before I know it, I feel the tenseness disappear and the weight melts from my shoulders. I have re-gained my centered-ness. Now I can once again look at the world squarely in the eye with an added bit of wisdom.

I can truly say that I've never found a person who was a better companion than solitude, of which Charles Cotton says: "The soul's best friend."

Contemplation is the Key

Key # 84 - Contemplation is the key to meditation.

We cannot meditate if we cannot contemplate. Focusing on the void (nothing) or on a pyramid with the vortex of light-energy in the middle, will enhance your silence and set a point of reference to quiet your mind. A simple decision to focus clearly, not to think, but to observe the passing of thoughts and not to get caught up in them until you have established a clear screen, is the most direct way to enter into a state of meditation.

Be careful not to allow yourself to be distracted by the emotions of past experiences that will accompany some of your thoughts. The process of meditation will take us into centers of the brain (the cerebellum) that will deliver new and improved programming. Every thought is a frequency that enters into our computer brain, and because we are constantly being fed by the great Cosmic Consciousness, receiving new information, we are always in a process of evolving.

This process of evolution varies for each of us. If we continue to run on old programs and do not allow ourselves to contemplate and silence the conscious mind—the neo-cortexes—we will evolve slower than those who consciously make time for meditating or creating this arena for engaging new programs through "imagery."

Neurological research and the science of physics confirm that our entire reality is realized through brain functions. We have known for centuries already, for example, that the sensation of sight is mainly taking place in the seeing centers of our brain rather than in the eye itself. Thus, meditation is the key to achieving a high level of success for tracking our self-worth and setting up new behavior patterns.

Emotions—Elements of a Quality Life

Key # 85 - When we become consciously aware of our emotions without judgment, we experience true love for ourselves and others.

In order to transcend those elements of life that seem invalidating but in their own way are stepping-stones to our ultimate state of bliss, we must become more open and aware of both beneficial and nullifying emotions. Once we are aware of these emotions, we can understand and accept them.

Vera, an 89-year-old dear client, is a spry individual who has come to recognize that depression is something she will not bring into her life. "I prefer not to listen to stories when people begin to talk about their problems and their depressed states of mind," she declares. "Negativity tends to deplete us of our vital energy. I'd much rather watch my Diamondbacks play baseball than listen to someone talk about their last operation!"

The ultimate dream is to stay neutral and not become excited or respond either positively or negatively to circumstances. These are simply polarities of the same thing. Stay out of judgment. Simply observe. Discernment is necessary for making decisions, but judgment is discriminatory. Judgment will stir emotions within you; it will trigger an attitude of self-defense. This is a feeling I'm sure you have experienced. It is a churning in the pit of your stomach, or solar plexus. This feeling is caused by an issue you have not yet resolved within yourself.

Practice Discernment

Discernment is a process of assessing a situation or circumstance without getting emotionally involved. Remember, emotions are ultimately our body's reactions towards our environment as a measure of response from our own neural pathways. In other words, they are a chemical/hormonal response throughout our body caused by our reaction to experiences, rather than pure "intent in action" or intention.

One might call discernment a detached observation that leads to objective evaluation. Once we come to understand the values of honesty, justice, self-respect and unity, we will recognize the difference between judgment and discernment.

Key # 86 - Judgment separates; discernment includes.

The establishing of a firm foundation upon which to build our life of quality and thus make better decisions, helps us to see the difference between judgment and discernment. Trust your intuition.

When we judge, we create unhealthy stress for ourselves. When we practice discernment, we merely acknowledge the difference between ourselves and another, or the difference between one situation and another without being emotionally involved. Practicing discernment allows us to make better choices.

Keep an Open Mind

Key # 87 - In a state of open-mindedness we can become tolerant of viewpoints and activities of others that may seem abusive and destructive.

If we take a closer look at the process of life, we discover that decay is a part of the life-giving processes. Likewise, seemingly destructive attitudes are necessary for growth and evolution of the whole. Tolerance without judgment, i.e., "detached openness" evokes compassion and love for everyone. It helps us to see "the one as all," or everyone as part of the same growing, evolving family.

Tranquility is a by-product of such compassion. Defined as serenity of spirit and stability of character, you do know when you have reached a state of tranquility! Whenever you are confronted by turmoil, confusion, despair and bewilderment of others, you will not be thrown off balance. You will maintain your gentleness of spirit and inner calm.

The Attitude of Gratitude

Key # 88 - A grateful heart is a peaceful one.

With gratitude in your life you will never experience lack. When you are in the state of constant gratitude you are already living in a state of abundance. All treasures and gifts of life are at your disposal—at your command. It only takes a reaching out to bring them into focus of the present experience. Hidden agendas of revenge, regret or victimization are in the hearts of those who exhibit lack, loss or any form of limitation.

Relaxation is the Crown for Meditation

In a relaxed state, you can more readily silence the mind and enter into a quiet receptive state.

Use the following system of relaxation to prepare yourself for meditation:

1. Physical comfort.
2. Eyes closed, or observing a candle flame.
3. Mind stops flitting from here to there.
4. Physical comfort increases to lethargy—no desire to move.
5. Breathing slows down and becomes deeper.
6. Feeling of heaviness from head to toe.
7. Feeling of detachment from surroundings.
8. Feeling in a "trance-like" state.
9. Ability to create listlessness.
10. Ability to open eyes or look around without affecting relaxation.

Accessing the Dynamo

I have found that one hour a day of uninterrupted silence refreshes my entire thought process and accesses the dynamo of power—the spark within—that sets me up for the day with clarity of purpose and direction. At the end of this chapter I'll give suggestions of ways to get yourself started with a regular meditation practice.

Key # 89 - Search for a source of self-knowledge outside ourselves only prolongs the process of growth.

Once you have created a path to your most Inner Self—subconscious mind, and you continue to travel this path on a regular basis, you will be amazed how effortlessly you can arrive at success and harmony in your life. By going within and spending time with your Self each day, you can bring forth that dynamo. Hundreds of my students have used meditation for accessing their inner power. In meditation you will discover your authentic Self: your steady flame of Being, that is different from your fluctuating personality or "daily-self"—the neo cortex.

Key # 90 - Combined daily activity and meditation, will deliver the quality life you are looking for.

When we have come to acquire our limitless power with the consciousness of our divinity, we will rarely feel tired or over-stressed. We will have the strength we've always desired.

Seven Steps to Getting Started on Your Meditation

Step # 1 - Select a place where you will not be interrupted for at least an hour. Sit down comfortably on a chair with both feet apart or sit on the floor in a yoga position (with a cushion under your seat only, your legs crossed in front of you). Close your eyes and take a deep breath through your nose. Exhale through your mouth after holding your breath briefly (keep your teeth together and force the breath out through your lips.) Take another deep breath again and exhale as before. Take a third deep breath and exhale again.

Many traditions emphasize the breath as one of the most valuable focal points for meditation. In the act of breathing all humans are connected to the Cosmic Consciousness—the Divine Mind. It is in the breath—the *prana*, that we remain alive. Thus, breathing plays an important role in our meditative efforts as well as in our daily life.

Step # 2 - Visualize yourself in your mental retreat, your favorite place for relaxation. This could be a place

in nature. Describe to yourself the details of your
sanctuary. Concentrate on the smallest of sounds and
finest of sensations. Actually hear the birds singing and
feel the warm summer sun on your skin; hear the gentle roar of the ocean waves, for example.

Step # 3 - Relax your entire body to the point of feeling
yourself rise above the floor or the chair. Become
calm, still and at peace. Allow your mind to drift
leisurely. Feel as though you are one with the universe.
Visualize the void or the pyramid—"fire in the middle."
Breathe steadily in a relaxed manner. Soon you will be
breathing very slowly. Relax your shoulders and neck,
allowing the rest of your body to follow.

Step # 4 - As you continue to breathe slowly, stop paying attention to your breathing and begin the count-
down: Ten ... nine ... count slowly down to one.
Concentrate on the colors of the rainbow. Slowly, one
by one, pause as you see each color completely in their
beauty and feel as if you "are" completely each color.
Take your time; bathe in each color entirely. See
the colors one by one: red ... orange ... yellow ...
Feel the different sensations as you become each different color ... green ... blue ... purple ... violet ...
Visualize a scene in each color, your own interpretation of that color. Become calm, still, at peace.

Step # 5 - Mentally create a large screen at a distance.
Make this screen as large as you would like; this is the
screen of your mind—the frontable lobe. Put a white
light around this screen; always focus scenes for your
screen with brilliant light upon them. Bring your imaginary retreat place onto the screen; embellish your picture with details. See yourself within this scene.

Step # 6 - Lovingly place your screen at the end of your imaginary studio or nesting place on a raised platform. Take another deep breath as you relax in your comfortable imaginary chair at your imaginary desk viewing your screen. Enjoy it while you are there. Count down: five ... four ... three ... two ... one. Take another deep breath slowly.

Step # 7 - Leisurely examine your workshop: chairs, computer, pictures, windows, plants, flowers, mountains, stream, ocean, etc. Install an imaginary assistant to whom you can turn for help. Visualize the possibilities of reaching anyone by phone—including anyone who has existed at any time. These could be great minds and thinkers of this universe. Blend with the beauty, love, wisdom and power you experience emanating from your imaginary characters. You are now ready to project onto your screen any situation you wish to study.

Other more direct subconscious mind contact meditation styles may be used. If interested in additional information about Ancient Wisdom of the Mayas, contact azodonnal@npgcable.com.

Tracking Questions

1. Where is consciousness? If you want to have a little fun with this question, look at a nearby wall and try to figure out where "you," the "inner self," the "looker," the "observer," are located. Then close both eyes and see how the location changes. Next, look with one eye at a time, and observe the movements. You will perceive the "self" moving around as you shift your visual apparatus.

2. How do blind people respond to this question?

3. Is meditation something you have been able to accomplish? Can you meditate in several different ways? List what you consider to be meditative states for yourself.

4. How often do you follow your "hunches"? Do you find that you are second guessing yourself? Do you find yourself asking for others' opinions before you make a decision?

5. In your conversations, can you come away from a confrontation without judgment?

6. Do you find yourself having hidden agendas when you do something for others? (Are you expecting appreciation, recognition, or the return of a favor?)

Tracking Exercises

Check yourself against the list below to find how close you are today with your meditation techniques. The column on the right leads to the column on the left.

If you experience	*then you can ...*
1. deeper and deeper body relaxation	improve your health
2. more tranquil mind relaxation	accelerate your success
3. clearer and clearer imagery	influence others enthusiastically
4. greater ability to create imaginary happenings as if they were real	attract the mate you prefer, create a flow of money
5. send your consciousness to other places	experience remote viewing
6. a "knowing" of what is happening anywhere	see ahead in time

Chapter 6

Breaking Old Patterns of Behavior

"... I know that within me is the intelligence to
understand and the power to overcome."

— Paramahansa Yogananda

Letting go of anything, including old patterns of behavior, often causes us to experience discomfort. Think about the queasiness you sometimes feel when you clean out your closet or throw away some knick-knacks that have been saved for so long. Did you like the twinge of disapproval you felt toward your spouse when they were going to get rid of something of yours while cleaning out the garage?

Even though we may know that letting go is an important aspect of experiencing life more fully, often that knowing doesn't ease the discomfort of actually doing it. You may want to hold onto these patterns because you've convinced yourself that it may be the best you will ever get. Doesn't that resemble those two twin has-beens, Lack 'n Loss?!!

How about trusting your ability to create something better for yourself? How about pretending "as if" you already had acquired the extra certification or training, or the new car, or the new relationship? How about getting excited about the wonderful surprises in store for you, once you let go of all that (empty) baggage?

A great master once said: "Refusal to change is devotion to ignorance." The great yogi, Paramahansa Yogananda wrote in his book, *Man's Eternal Quest*: "Ignorance is the supreme disease." Let us not be caught up in this debilitating disease.

You may want to begin by letting go of the attitudes and behaviors that are not bringing precise or peaceful results. Perhaps it would be best to start with the release of roles such as "victim" or "savior." Both roles are polarity symptoms.

You may start with letting go of a relationship, job, or even a way of life that no longer serves your purpose; thus, unlocking the realms of the divine within you and enjoying its treasures.

Key # 91 - Letting go of these attitudes will require a firm and steady commitment to taking time for solitude and introspection.

At the end of each day, take time to review your outlook on everything that transpired from the time you awoke, to that moment. Find a quiet place before you retire, and write down your thoughts and observations in a journal. Review your actions during the past day. Ask questions.

Remember, the answers are within you. All you need to do is "be still and listen." Continue to practice silencing your mind.

Old Patterns of Behavior Have Hidden Roots

I'm sure you've found yourself sometimes wondering why you do things a certain way. Are there habits you find yourself repeating, or situations that keep coming up for you that have you puzzled? If you have been practicing some of these for a long time, you may even have forgotten how habitual they really are.

Key # 92 - Most of the patterns of behavior that are no longer useful have a built-in self-sabotaging mechanism.

Robert is an example of a person who was sabotaging himself but didn't know it. He would come to the salon occasionally just to chat, and I soon learned that he considered himself capable of making sound decisions. However, he never seemed to have enough money to pay his bills. He did want to live well, but somehow he never managed to stay above the level of survival.

Robert had no difficulty finding a job, but eventually he would quit, usually because he was ill or had a previous engagement.

Darlene was another friend who was resistant to changing her behavior patterns even though they worked against her. She was a good friend to others and did all sorts of favors for everyone except herself. She was a wonderful babysitter, would cook gourmet meals for her boyfriend, drive her neighbor to another town, requiring a full day of driving that put her behind with her own work, etc. Darlene was always there for everyone except herself, and then she wondered why she never seemed to be caught up, and why she never seemed to accomplish what she had set out to do.

Cory was married five times to five men who abused her. She did not understand that the root of her dilemma lay not with her husbands and the way they treated her, but with herself. In fact, she was literally asking for the abuse they dished out.

Buried deep within, Cory eventually discovered insecurity, lack of self-forgiveness, abandonment, judgment and the inability to love or even like herself. She then realized that until she changed her attitudes and outlooks toward herself and her life—until she released the old patterns, she would continue to attract men who matched her feelings of insecurity and low self-esteem. Blaming her husbands for her own shortcomings only empowered them.

Remember: You empower the person, substance or circumstance that you blame.

Determine the usefulness of the attitudes and conduct that have enslaved you. If you sincerely wish to delete these patterns in your present life, you can. Remember, you chose those patterns and embedded them in your unconscious mind so they would continue to work for you. Now you are learning how to quickly and permanently remove them.

Perhaps in your unconscious past, you did not understand that they delivered some form of "payoff" that you wanted or felt you needed, or you wouldn't have adopted them in the first place.

Ask yourself: What am I getting in return for holding onto this pattern? Could there be a better payoff than that one? Such as: finally being able to buy that new home or new car; or finally being able to find a partner who is loving, caring, productive and fun to be with. Such as: finally getting to enjoy myself, enjoy the work I do that delivers the money I need— and more—in order to have the comforts I have always wanted. Such as: having the body shape and weight I have always desired, and being able to maintain a healthy, robust lifestyle that brings a glow to my cheeks and a shine to my hair.

Bob is a bright, accomplished individual in his early 40s. He has his life pretty much well under his belt. One day when he came into the salon for a haircut, he seemed quieter than usual.

"Hey, Bob, a little cold today, isn't it?" I made friendly conversation.

"In more ways than one." he retorted.

"Do you care to tell your favorite 'psychopractor' about it?" I quipped.

"You are certainly that," he smiled, sighing heavily. "You've used your magic on my attitude before, so I challenge you to go for it again."

"I guess my reputation for giving people attitude adjustments follows me wherever I go. But I'll be gentle with you," I grinned.

"I've actually allowed myself to get taken in by other people's comments and this has led to making some unwise decisions lately in the stock market," Bob shook his head, "and now I find myself being eaten up by that ugly worm of fear."

"Ahh ... you remembered what I called it in the past." I placed a towel around his shoulders as he sat down in the chair.

"You need to give me one good word of advice and I think I can handle it from there." Bob eyed me in the mirror.

"This one will be short and sweet, just like your haircut," I chuckled. "Each one of us is like a star in the heavens. If we stay in our true orbit, withstanding the winds of change, remaining true to the nature of our being, we will continue to shine and not fall to the tug of another's gravitational pull."

"That's what you call short?" Now it was Bob's turn to chuckle. "It will take me till my next haircut to chew on that one!" I already knew that Bob would ask himself those honest questions that would allow him to move forward with confidence. Apparently, others had started to pull his strings, or pull him off orbit. He only needed someone to help him become aware of his recent "wobble" and its origin.

The Alter Ego has to Go

Key # 93 - In the process of switching from one frame of reference to another, you will find yourself dealing with your ego.
This is not as challenging as you may think. In fact, you may be grateful for the intervention.

Perhaps there is nothing more misunderstood in our world than the term "ego." You have an ego in order to identify your self, or who you are, in the natural element. It is the "altered" ego, or alterations we impose on our ego that cause it to go into a spin. The ego is the strength you are born with. The "altered" ego, if you let it, can create the illusions of security, grandeur and superiority over others. As soon as you remove the imposter who has tried to take over the throne of your being, you will empower the true king and queen.

Myra, whom I nicknamed "Princess," is a sales representative for a beauty supply company. She is a beautiful young woman. Her serene eyes made you feel loved, and you know from the gentleness of her speech that she is generous, warm, caring and kind. Her products are good, so I often buy them.

Shortly after Myra had moved to Phoenix, she met Rick, who had become her boyfriend for the past six months. One day, as she was tallying up the purchase order for the month's items, Myra paused and looked up at me. "Rick dumped me for another girl."

"Really?" was my uninvolved answer.

"He came over the other night." she continued looking at me across my desk, "and he told me he knew my game." From previous conversations I also was aware that Myra did have a "game," or payoff from her behavior towards men.

"You tend to act so nice and caring toward guys initially, but you change after a while." I responded.

"You noticed that?" She opened her eyes wider and stared at me in amazement.

"I could tell from the stories you tell me."

Myra sat for a few minutes without saying anything. "What do I do to change that? I don't want to end up being an old maid!" she declared.

"First of all," I told her, "you must find out why you act so nice and then later turn on them."

"My gosh, I guess I change because then I 'have' them. I know they're mine." She shook her head sorrowfully. "I want to be different now!"

"You must understand that each action you take in life is representative of an act of love, with intent to unite with the other person. You must determine if you are choosing to act a certain way because you are expecting a certain return from that action. You have to be true to your nature and true to the nature of the other party concerned." I smiled quietly at her, as a shadow crossed over her face.

"I don't understand."

"You will," I reassured her, "when you take the time to be honest with yourself and eliminate the need for a payoff in your behavior." I handed her a check for the items I'd purchased and stepped out of the office with her.

"I'll be back next week for the next chapter," said Myra, following after me.

"First take a week to meditate and ask yourself about the things I said. Then we'll talk again." I gave her a hug. "Goodbye, Princess!"

Mark is another person who did a turn-around when his behavior was becoming self-serving. In his early 30s, well-dressed and self-assured, Mark came in regularly for bi-monthly haircuts. He liked to boast about his debonair manner and about how he was in "the in" with the single gals.

Bob would often tell me, "If I didn't say the things I say to those girls, they wouldn't come onto me."

"Is that the way you see it?" I asked casually one day.

"Of course! Don't you think it's necessary to have a line to get what you want?"

"Yes, I suppose so," I responded. "If those are the results you want in life, that is the best way to do it."

"Why do you say it that way?" He frowned, tipping his head to one side, ready to listen.

"I say it that way because that is the way you talk to others. So, this is the only way you will understand me. You carry on a conversation with hidden agendas to receive something back in return, and you really are not being very caring of the gals any further than to get what you want. Is that not so?" I stopped what I was doing and waited for his response.

"Man, you really know how to hurt a guy!" retorted Mark. Silently I continued his haircut. "Well, I guess I have to examine my intentions and stop being so selfish," he said at length.

"If you want different results, you do," I responded firmly.

He looked at himself in the mirror, got off the chair and stepped over to the reception desk in silence. "I'm getting sort of tired of this single life," he said sheepishly, taking out his wallet and avoiding my eyes. "Maybe doing things in a different way will bring the right gal."

"Mark," I smiled at him, "you'll know when the time is ripe for Mr. Right to attract the right gal. You'll figure it out. What do you think?"

Key # 94 - Hidden agendas in any relationship eventually deliver pain.

Consider the "payoffs" for your current behavior patterns. Do they really deliver what you want from life, or is it time to consider different rewards—such as self-esteem, serenity, a sense of loyalty to your inner values, and a feeling that you are finally on the bright path for achieving your full self-worth?

Sometimes it is not easy to know when a behavior has become a habit. It is not easy to know that you have actually become addicted to acting a certain way or having the same attitude toward similar circumstances in order to receive the expected or predictable payoff.

There is always some form of reward for the efforts you put forth. The key is to ask yourself what your intentions are. Then ask if there might be a better payoff that would be even more rewarding than the one that has become locked in place by patterned behavior or habits.

Do You Need to Change Some of These Patterns?

Key # 95 - Closing the door on the excitement of life is an indication that your energy is stuck in the disappointments of the past.

Pessimists and others who lack enthusiasm or zest for life usually are consumed by unfulfilled longing for the past. The inability to overcome grief for loved ones is another sign of holding onto attitudes that are depleting that person's energy reserves. Usually these people will have difficulty conducting everyday affairs with ease. They will be overcome by the inability to concentrate and eventually become sluggish. The senses become numbed and they tend to want to sleep a lot, and avoid the freshness of a sunny day. They may close the blinds in their bedroom and turn off the phone to avoid calls.

Thinking becomes more of a reactive attitude in which they will tend to rationalize situations and relationships. If you find yourself getting bored with life in general; if you do not become excited about the little things of life, such as watching birds or listening to the laughter of children, you have purchased a ticket to despair.

If idleness and slothfulness are part of your picture, you have begun the roller-coaster ride of a mind that will play tricks on you. If you have been treading water and find that feelings of self-motivation have abandoned you, you are in the throes of back-tracking into outdated patterns of behavior and poisoned thoughts.

Temporary fixes and addictive behavior are merely a dependency on "payoffs" that have the illusion of producing the rewards you are looking for. Instead, they usually lead to debilitating or dysfunctional behavior. Unwillingness to get involved usually comes with a host of excuses, often expertly contrived.

Here is a list of other patterns of behavior that often hold people back:

- Indecisiveness
- Arguing with others
- Feeling worse after you become angry
- Getting along poorly with others
- Irritability
- Stubbornness
- Rash behavior
- Contrary-ness
- Emotional outbursts

• Mood swings
• Suppressing your emotions
• Angering easily
• Easily agitated and distressed
• Jealousy
• Gossiping

Retreating to Solitude

Key # 96 - If you can remember that everything you experience in your life you have personally created, you will be more understanding and forgiving of yourself.

In your retreat, that special place where you are now spending at least twenty minutes each day, you will start to feel comfortable about yourself, more forgiving. At first, however, your new feelings may feel strange, as if they don't quite fit.

Remember when you were a child breaking in a new pair of shoes? Or even as an adult, if you are an athlete, breaking in new running or tennis shoes ... At first they feel like someone else's until they start to conform to your foot and your way of walking or running in them.

When you try on these new patterns—these gems of wisdom, you may not be able to discern which "you" is your true self. Gradually you will gather confidence, and these new feelings of worthiness will deliver the peace you are seeking in your special retreat. You will also start to harvest clarity and abundance. Take responsibility for your actions and attitudes, and experience only that which you prefer!

Annette had a habit of re-acting to other people's comments about her body weight. She knew she could often hide these uncomfortable feelings and she pretended that she didn't care about their comments. In reality however, she was deeply hurt.

Annette wanted to change her attitude about herself and the uncomfortable response to the judgment of others. One day, as I was giving her a new hair style, I also gave her a new idea about how to begin her modification. She started by setting aside ten minutes every evening to be by herself, in solitude. At first she found it difficult to quiet her mind and her emotions. She also continued to re-live the same emotions that caused discomfort.

Then, after three days, she noticed she was beginning to see herself as a silent observer of her daily activities and conversations. She didn't seem to be so emotionally affected by the events she was reviewing.

Annette was beginning her new life style by releasing the attachment to her most recent past. Eventually she was able to initiate the removal of her outdated deep-seated dispositions. She discovered that her emotions were simply personalized thoughts reacting to her own ideas. It was these thoughts that had materialized and caused comments by others about her weight. They were verbalized hidden ideas she had about herself.

In her solitude Annette started to get to know herself. Her own inner light was holding up a mirror to herself in order to give her greater self-understanding. Her physiological symptoms of fear—the inconspicuous tightening of her fists, sudden heart palpitations and twinges that caused knots in her stomach were a part of her uncontrolled responses to her habitual disposition toward her extra body weight.

Annette discovered that loving herself and becoming her own best friend gave her a feeling of peace and a different attitude toward her body and its appearance. Soon her weight was normal and her health remarkable.

Annette had tapped into the inner core of her being with an attitude of self-acceptance and love. These new feelings caused her to behave differently toward herself, and her habits changed radically. Soon she had more energy and she enjoyed the feeling of "being in" her body.

Viewpoints Can Be a Snag

Key # 97 - Your viewpoints and preference for doing things a certain way, will be two of the most difficult "attachments" to release.

Letting go of your opinions is not always easy. When you insist on holding onto these viewpoints, you deplete much of your precious energy.

Take the time in your solitude to meditate on attitudes, outlooks and opinions and ask yourself if they suit your highest sense of joy. Do they resonate with your list of values and priorities? Often these viewpoints may be deeply embedded in your lifestyle and behavior patterns. You may not realize how dependent you have become on "having things a certain way."

As you study these viewpoints, examine how they may be subtly depleting your energy and eating away at your peace of mind. Write down in your journal how you will go about altering these subtle preferences. Start practicing non-attachment by taking one thing at a time.

For instance, consider the way you like to arrange your towels on the bathroom racks; how you arrange your tools on your workbench; how you place the dishes in the dishwasher, if you have one. Consider the route you prefer to take to work, or the way you organize your closets.

You may not realize that you are emotionally connected to doing or having things a certain way. In fact, you may be so attached to these inclinations, you may feel a certain discomfort or stirring inside that stabs at your composure if you notice something "out of place," "done wrong," or "just not right."

Evaluate these dependencies. What would happen, for example, if someone placed the dishes differently in your dishwasher? What would happen if the towels were crooked on the racks? What if your screwdrivers and nails were on the left instead of the right side of your workbench?

To begin changing your dependency on matters that you may discover are so insignificant that you cannot find any serious reasons for experiencing uncomfortable twinges when others may deal with them differently, you may wish to put the silverware up instead of down in the dishwasher yourself. You may wish to take a different route to work.

The point to remember is: You do not have to give up your inclinations. Focus on surrendering your dependency on them. This is the way to consciously build flexibility into your life.

Doris was ten minutes away from the salon, under ordinary traffic circumstances. On that day, however, there was an accident that caused a backup of traffic. She had an appointment with me at 1 PM and she was running late anyway.

Doris was frantic, especially since she did not have the salon phone number logged into her cell phone, so she couldn't call me to tell me she'd be late. She tried to call her sister, who would have the salon phone number, but she wasn't home.

When she arrived a half hour late, Doris was exhausted and felt so guilty, she couldn't stop apologizing.

"Never worry," I reassured her. "Things have a way of working out for the best for everyone involved."

"I never like someone to be late to an appointment with me, so I know how you must feel. I'm so sorry," Doris kept repeating.

"Relax!" I smiled. "I'll simply call my next client and tell her to come a little later. I have some extra time this afternoon. Tell yourself the universe is perfect and there are no failures," I reassured her, placing a call to Kathy, my next client.

"Oh dear," Kathy answered the phone. "I guess I forgot to call to cancel my appointment today. "The baby's sick and I have to take her to the doctor."

"Wow, I guess you're right." Doris shook her head, eying me in wonderment ... as if this little "sample example of universal order" was all my doing!

Give yourself the gift of detaching from worries, and trust that you are creating everything perfectly. Trust in the divine order of the universe.

Too often we forget to be fully aware of what is really taking place at the moment we are having an experience. We need to remember that we bring certain circumstances into our lives to awaken us to our great power within.

We create relationships and circumstances to reap more self-knowledge. This allows us to enhance our self-worth, or increase the value we place on every aspect of our life: our thoughts, emotions, behaviors, habits, actions, attitudes, viewpoints, opinions ... All of these aspects are grist for the mill.

Be aware and receptive. You will be amazed how much you will learn from even the smallest and seemingly insignificant experience. Once we "give up the fight" and let go of the feeling that we have become the victim of circumstances, we give ourselves the opportunity to evolve more rapidly from consciously determining to listen to our inner voice. From this conscious decision to grow and relish our experiences, we reap the benefits of discernment.

Self-knowledge, self-worth and personal empowerment emerge when we ask: "Why did I create this?" "What is the purpose for this experience?" and, "What am I to learn from this?"

As we go within to seek the answers, we learn to respect and trust our intuition. You will find that as you make a habit of going with your hunches—getting favorable results—you will establish a sense of self-trust. This will lead to feelings of inner harmony.

How to Remain Calm in Emergencies

How do you respond to emergencies? Do you become defensive, protective or accusative/informative? What would happen if you were driving down the street, a child ran in front of your car and you had to slam on the brakes to keep from hitting her?

What would be your first reaction? Do you become defensive of your rights? Do you react to the child's needs and become protective? Or do you accuse the parent and start to deliver a diatribe about the need to teach the child some safety rules?

In order to remove yourself from your strong opinions, first you have to decide if you do indeed wish to detach from your re-active mode. It is wise to let go of becoming emotionally attached to emergency situations; thus taking a neutral, non-judgmental, loving attitude. This may sound absurd when you are in the midst of major chaos, such as a fire, hurricane, car accident, sudden illness, etc.

Yet, if you can distance yourself from the emergency and know that everything is in divine order, you will sail through any crisis without being emotionally affected. A built-in bonus is also in store for you: As you continue to detach yourself from these "crises," their impact will diminish ... along with the number of crises. You will have fewer "911" situations. I call this "winning the war and emerging without any battle scars"!

Can You Keep Yourself from Saying Something?

Detachment from strong negative emotions is another stepping stone toward achieving full self-worth. Anger, resentment, disappointment and despair are examples of harmful strong emotions that rob you of your energy and leave you feeling depleted.

Calmly and without judgment, observe what is going on around you. Decide to keep your mouth shut! Having an observer's attitude toward others and their own experiences releases you from their dramas.

Drew, one of my favorite clients, told me his story one hot summer day: "I pulled it off this last time," he declared as he thumbed through an issue of *Sports Illustrated*. "I really bit my tongue and listened to what she had to say."

"You mean you didn't bark back at your wife because she was going to her mom's in Pennsylvania?" I stopped cutting his hair and looked him directly.

"Yup, I actually let her tell me her reasons for going. And—you know something? They actually made sense." He eyed me directly with his clear blue eyes.

"I think that's wonderful," I exclaimed.

"Yup, it made me feel better than I expected. I felt love for my mother-in-law too," he chuckled.

"Wow, how amazing!" I winked at him.

We both had nothing more to say. Empowerment is a serenity that comes only as you taste the sweetness of silence in wisdom.

When you have come to recognize your impetuous involvement in a situation, you will know why detachment is necessary. Taking the first step in identifying these emotions creates a strong desire for change. Once you make the necessary changes, you will never lack for energy; nor will you lose any more of your energy. Like Drew, you will feel empowered.

Let Go Of an Illusory Image

Key # 98 - Detaching from the need to have things work out in a certain way—"your way"—indicates progress in your stability of living in the present moment.

When you live in a blissful state, it is easier to detect where and when you are getting stuck in the past. You realize how encumbered you are by an image of yourself rather than the true picture. This image can take on all sorts of costumes and wear a variety of hats.

Key # 99 - Willingness to detach from what others think of you is another indication of coming in contact with your own true self-image.

Karla, the girl next door, shared a story with me one day when we were both outside tending to our yard.

"I wanted to kill him!" Angrily Karla pulled out the weeds from under the bushes she had just finished trimming.

I put down my pruning shears and eyed her directly.

"Ted pulled out of the garage this morning and ran over a flat of flowers I had left in the garage," she exploded.

"Did he know they were there?" I asked.

"Well ... I guess he didn't know; I had left them too close to the truck and he couldn't see them."

"It's not quite so bad, is it? You can always replace a flat of flowers. The difficult part is replacing your pride—right?" I joked with her as I closed the garbage can lid over my rose bush prunings.

"Umm. I can let go of that awful feeling I had when I first saw that ruined flat of flowers lying there. I'm slowly working on letting go of my need for his approval. Sometimes I take it out on him. I guess the past is harder to get rid of than these weeds," she admitted.

"Take it easy on yourself." I gave Karla a hug. "The best intentions sometimes come snapping back at you, but the past will never haunt you when you pay attention to your feelings."

"I'm sorry I wrapped you up in my stuff," Karla apologized. "I remember the last time we were out here in the yard, you told me to keep my mind open to new things and not to allow the past to take me off track."

I looked up at the noisy birds in the trees and mused, "If only we could remain as happy as the birds, fluttering from moment to moment, leaving the past to yesterday and without a care about the opinions of others ..."

Upgraded Models Frighten Others

Key # 100 - If you find yourself associating regularly with those who are attached to other people's opinions and you base some of your actions and decisions on their approval or validation, this is an indication of your own attachment to others' opinions.

Did you ever radically change your hairstyle or mode of dress so that suddenly people took special notice? You may elicit the same response from others as you now start to change your attitudes, outlooks, behaviors and habits. They are so accustomed to dealing with the Former You. Suddenly they feel as though they're talking with a stranger.

You can't very well say, "That's okay, Susan, I've just upgraded my model—you'll get used to it in time!" After all, how do you know that? They may have wanted you to remain a victim or a person who feels unworthy of independence, success, happiness and its rewards. Others may have thrived on your dependencies and feelings of low esteem.

What if you lose the friendship of some of these people? Does this really matter to you, in your new state of being? Do you still need to be liked, appreciated or understood by others? Let go of these attachments. They no longer serve your goal of achieving self-love and self-esteem. In your moments of mediation, in that safe place you have created for yourself, you are coming to experience a deeper sense of who you really are and why you are here. You are discovering that your potential is much greater when you are not bound by what others think of you.

Advancing yourself to the point where you do not need praise or validation by others delicately carries you into that desirable state of serenity. Accepting comfortably the fact that other people have reactions to what you do, thrusts you across the abyss into the realm of your divine power within. You grow strong from the value you give to your own work because you are you viewing it from the perspective of your internal sense of worth. You are participating in the experience of your creative mind in action.

Give yourself the gift of detaching from your worries, and trust that you are creating everything perfectly.

Detachment Does Not Mean That You Don't Love Others

Key # 101 - Removing yourself from other people's dramas and issues does not mean that you don't care.

In our culture we have been led to believe that if we detach from others we do not care about them or love them. Removing yourself from their "stuff" does not mean that you don't care. Actually it means that you are more intensely involved in caring because you are more awakened and evolved in your understanding.

You might think that the suffering others are experiencing could end rapidly; or you might feel that their lives would be less complicated if they were willing to let go and make certain different decisions. You now can have a compassionate heart toward them, but you now know that they need to work out their situations through their own experiences. You realize how important it is to let them experience their own drama in order to achieve the awareness and awakening that will give them the insights they seek on their life's journey.

Some of you may ask, "If I do away with my feelings about the way others view me, won't I become numb altogether, to the feelings of others?" This is a question you must answer yourselves, by applying what you have now proven works for yourself. I do know, however, that you will find much more joy and inner peace when you release your attachments.

Your world will expand and new opportunities will present themselves for you to put into practice your new-found knowledge. Remember, knowledge becomes wisdom when you successfully apply it to every situation you encounter in your daily life.

Key # 102 - Becoming detached will give you freedom and energy you never dreamed could be yours.

Your expanded awareness will allow you to become aware of your ability to more keenly feel the pleasant response of your senses. What once was a dull and pent-up mindfulness liberates itself. You will declare: "I am free! I am not afraid!" You will have a sense of freedom and well-being, regardless of the thoughts, actions and opinions of others.

Joan was a woman of courage, but she hid behind her intellect. In the winter months when she visited Arizona from Rhode Island, she used to come to the salon every week. She spent these months in Arizona alone, apart from the rest of her family. We talked often about the flak she received from the family because of her decision to winter in a warm climate, away from them.

"At first I could not bring myself to leaving my home and its comforts back in Rhode Island," she said one day.

"What helped you to change your mind?" I asked her.

"I suppose I can attribute it to recognizing that I was afraid of change and of what others might say if I didn't spend the holidays with my family," she admitted. "That fear was freezing me up more than the weather was," she chuckled. "It all has a lot to do with accepting change, and knowing that you can be away from family and still love them, doesn't it?"

Key # 103 - *It is the act of letting go, that crowns your attitude of trust.*

When you are fulfilled by a sense of trust, you are happy. You exhibit characteristics of a person who is both physically and mentally healthy.

Although you are discovering how nice you have been to yourself, sometimes you may find yourself asking: "Am I nice to myself because I'm happy, or am I happy because I'm nice to myself?" To help you determine the answer to that illusive question, here are some questions you could ask yourself:

- Did I let people take advantage of me?
- Did I allow unresolved anger and/or resentment to hurt any of my relationships?
- Did I overreact to other people's comments and opinions, making a difficult situation even worse?
- Did I become angry and/or frustrated when dealing with difficult people?
- Did I ever feel trapped in a seemingly unresolved conflict?

Your answers will give you a clue to what you have changed and learned to abolish in your life; thus leading you into a more joyful life experience.

Detachment Helps to Solve Conflicts

Key # 104 - Strength comes in knowing you are not affected by others.

You will be surprised how non-attachment aids you in solving conflicts. Your strength will come in knowing you are not affected emotionally by others, and by applying what you have discovered about yourself. Once you realize there are three sides to every conflict—people, issues and neutral position—and you deal with them effectively, you will know you have established a lifestyle that is more fitting to the way you wish to live.

Knowing yourself and understanding that your own personality traits are a part of your unique way of dealing with conflict and difficult situations and people, allow you to choose the words you will use to remain non-judgmental when conversing with others. This begins the process of resolving situations you would like to release. When you are honest and use detached understanding when communicating with challenging or conflicted individuals, it will help you to keep your cool, stay neutral and execute a wise solution.

Where Are You with the "Bigger Picture"?

In your new way of thinking and living, you have established a certain quality of energy around yourself. This energy's vibration acts as a magnet to attract others who share the same values and who also desire to be independent, empowered and successful in their endeavors.

These people will be a support system that will assist you on your journey. Having family, friends and/or co-workers as an emotional support system helps you build your strength and engenders feelings of validity. It also makes you feel part of a greater whole.

In my own family, we take time to connect with each other on a regular basis. Since there are at least six or seven of us who will initiate personal visits to other members of the family, it has become a natural occurrence to visit, talk and discuss episodes that take us through life into other dimensions of existence. It is not uncommon for us to sleep over or to stay up all night reviewing occurrences and learning to dissect them for the purpose of extracting from them the "moral of the story."

Hobbies Provide a "Growing Field"

Key # 105 - Engaging in a hobby is a way of keeping yourself happy.

How do you like to spend your time? Perhaps this time is mainly aligned with the way you earn your living. Or it may involve activities to which there is no earning power attached. I consider my artful work in the beauty business a hobby. It affords me a comfortable arena for sharing my knowledge, offering a service of love in my endeavors, and interacting on a daily basis with others. I also enjoy educating others to a happier life in my weekly gatherings and monthly retreats.

It is crucial to your growth to establish arenas and fields of ease. These will empower you with the will to take risks, grow in knowledge and receive the rewards of the wisdom from application of that knowledge. A hobby provides this arena because you are passionate about it and therefore, you feel no need or desire to defend it.

Trod Often upon the New Paths in Your Neural-Net

Key # 106 - We establish neural-net connections through repeated patterns of behavior.

In the neural-net of our brains, we easily follow these patterns. Therefore, to delete the unwanted routes of these minute electrical connections and re-pattern the mind, we must repeatedly and deliberately travel the new neural pathways we are establishing.

I like to compare the re-programming process to the planting of a garden. After you have planted your garden of fruit trees and vegetables you can sit back and allow them to produce their crop. The radishes and strawberries come up sooner than the carrots or oranges; that's all right. Give every fruit and vegetable their natural time to produce. Enjoy the rhythm of nature. Eat your radishes and strawberries, knowing that soon you will have oranges and apples.

Oh, by the way, where did you get the seeds for the trees in the first place? Your neighbor brought over some fruit and you enjoyed their crop, saving the seeds. Now it is time to share strawberries in exchange for oranges until your trees come to bear fruit!! Note how everything has its natural cycle and is enveloped in the beauty of loving-kindness.

Don't forget to water your garden. Nurture the neural pathways from which you wish to harvest.

Remember to allow enough time for the physical part of yourself to re-route and re-charge. In your mind you already may have the patterns in place, but the physical "caboose" takes awhile to arrive when the train has a long string of passenger cars traveling behind it. Freedom is a process, not a product.

Establishing a new life style will come in time. Your ability to say "no" without guilt to situations that used to plague you, will be a daily occurrence. Your rewards will be inner serenity and peace of mind. You will find yourself with extraordinary reserves of strength that enable you to enjoy life to its fullest. Who would not love to live in such a state of mind?

Key # 107 - Live your days in serenity, in the midst of seeming chaos.

An English psychologist, F.W. Myers said: "Hidden in the deep of your being is a rubbish heap as well as a treasure house." It is up to us to find that treasure house within; to bear the "rubbish" and then toss it aside.

Taking the First Step

Here are six insights to remember on the road to non-attachment:

1. Evaluate your strong preferences. They exist in your life in subtle ways.
2. Center yourself. Become keenly aware of your self-worth and of how you are creating your experiences; where is the fine print?
3. Detach from needing praise or validation. Trust your own worth. When something comes up that stirs your emotions, stop; remember your "new and improved" skills and apply them.
4. Appreciate others in their present expression. If they do not align with you, bless them and let them reside in their chosen space; go on with your own creations. Do not get sucked into their dramas.
5. Invite your friends to play at your own level of consciousness. Some may stay and play, but others may leave. Become aware of your changes. When your experiences involve someone else, know that both of you have agreed to participate in the drama together.
6. Trust that things are happening for the best—divine order is in command. You are responsible for all that you experience. With this awareness, your life will become more effective.

Tracking Questions

1. How comfortable are you with letting go of the need for validation (about your opinions and beliefs) from others?
2. What is the fear you might have about not pleasing others?

3. Which do you dislike most:
   a) not being understood
   b) not being appreciated
   c) not being liked?
4. What do you feel is one of your strongest attachments with your family?
5. From what preference are you willing to detach today?
6. Do you feel responsible for making other people's lives work? Are you willing to change that feeling?

Six Mental Exercises

1. List three of your strongest viewpoints or opinions, i.e., about the way you feel about those who don't say "thank you," about the way some people drive, etc.
2. List three things you are willing to completely release.
3. Create a schedule for establishing moments of silence, for periods of twice a day.
4. List two strong attachments that you will release, just for one day, in order to learn to eventually detach from them completely.
5. Note how your hobby is a comfortable arena for your development. Make an outline of how you will play your new role.
6. Write a short sentence that describes your understanding of your neural-net connections and how they affect your changes.

Chapter 7

Happiness: A Product of Discipline

"Happiness is a butterfly which, when pursued, is always just beyond your grasp, but which, if you will sit down quietly, may alight upon you."

— Nathaniel Hawthorne

The physical universe, energy in motion, is magnetic and electric. It is magical! This life force energy is the power of creating. Since creations are conceived by thoughts (energy in motion), they usher in any number of possibilities to be experienced.

Key # 108 - By choice and with discipline, the creative life force energy can produce what we call happiness—a path that leads to the greatest treasure—your electromagnetic light within.

Even though the hidden power of this energy is not well known to ordinary man, scientists have discovered some of its mysteries. Using newly developed highly sensitive instruments, researchers in De La Warr laboratories in England have detected patterns of electromagnetic power that surround the human body. They discovered that these electromagnetic patterns changed with the person's thoughts.

Incredible! Magical! Yet, little understood.

135

A polygraph expert conducted another interesting study with plants that demonstrates the immensity of electromagnetic power. In his book, *The Secret Life of Plants*, Peter Tompkins writes that thought wave energy is everywhere. Even the keen frequencies of plants can detect it. In his curiosity to learn more about the ability of plants to react to the electromagnetic wave patterns of human thought, he placed electrodes on a plant in his office. He began by touching the leaves and observing the recordings on the polygraph. Soon he noticed curious patterns on the polygraph printouts.

Tompkins decided to further test his plant. Stimulated by the results, he wondered what would happen if he were to dip one of the leaves into his cup of coffee. To his amazement, he found that his plant recorded a marked reactive activity *before* he had a chance to place the leaf in the hot coffee. His plant had reacted to his thoughts!

If plants can read thoughts, what are thoughts? asked Tompkins. How do thoughts affect our lives? Are we indeed the creators of our destiny through our thoughts? How does this electromagnetic energy in motion play a part in what we call happiness?

Electromagnetism is a Creative Power

Thoughts, the force that reflects our principles and echoes our discipline, are the same electromagnetic energies that were picked up by the plants of Hopkins' experiment. Thoughts are powerful and creative.

Key # 109 - Through spoken words our thoughts bring about a world of defined results.

Depending on how selective we are with our words, the outcome of thoughts can be a creation of happiness or a life of despair.

Key # 110 - Disciplined activity of monitored thoughts gives us freedom and delivers happiness.

This discipline gives us autonomy and sovereignty. Autonomy is independence that claims personal governorship. It means we are in control of the outcome of experiences that we have consciously and deliberately created. Since our actions communicate who we are to others, self-control develops out of a conscious effort to cultivate and monitor the thoughts that will be delivered by our words.

You may not believe that what you think, say and feel really does create your future. If you monitor your thoughts for a day or two, however, you will soon discover yourself as the author of your destiny. You will clearly see how your thoughts have been spoken and how they have been the instigators of feelings. The simple exercise with a daily schedule we did in Chapter Three quickly demonstrates this:

Make or buy a weekday calendar with hourly slots for each day. Track your thoughts by writing in each slot the dominating idea in your mind for each hour. You will discover a pattern of what takes precedence in your mind and you will find how your life has been governed by them. Surprised?

Since our words and actions are predestined by our thoughts and feelings, they echo who we are. It is necessary to carefully monitor ourselves in order to become more aware of how we are forecasting our destiny. Once we gain autonomy we realize more self-discipline. Through self-discipline we discover the magic of living out our dreams. Our world becomes filled with more happiness and we live longer.

The Pursuit of Happiness

In our own U.S. Declaration of Independence our founding fathers considered "the pursuit of happiness" important enough to include as a part of our inalienable rights.

What does that "happiness pursuit" look like to most Americans? Often they presume that material gain brings this happiness, so they focus their energy and attention on acquiring a richly-furnished house, expensive vehicle, boat, large wardrobe, jewelry, vacation home, etc. These acquisitions may indeed provide much pleasure at the same time they seem not to address the requirements for happiness. This frustration has led many people down the twisted roads of confusion and a life of coping that destroys their ability to seek true happiness.

What is happiness? According to the philosopher, Nietzsche, it is "the feeling that power increases—that resistance is overcome." Ingrid Bergman states: "Happiness lies in good health and a bad memory." Bertrand Russell found happiness to be tranquility of mind. Aristotle considered it to be a matter of being virtuous. Benjamin Franklin stresses moderation of pleasures as the source of happiness.

With so many definitions and opinions about what happiness may be, how does one *really* know what it is and where to find it?

Perhaps the answer to this loaded question is simply: You know that you are happy because you feel it. It sings throughout your very being.

It has been my conscious pursuit for over 35 years to intentionally create a life of jubilation in spite of the many obstacles that would dictate otherwise. Those who know me well attest to my exuberance, my peace of mind and my zealous pursuit of happiness. That is why I am writing this book. I want to share with others what I have learned about happiness and how to achieve it.

Key # 111 - Contentment is a personal choice, an inner peace.

In his book, *Happiness Is A Choice*, Barry Neil Kaufman says, "Each of us ... accesses an amazing attitude advantage within ourselves once we come to know that happiness ... is a choice and misery is optional ..."

Happiness is something we can all access at any time. Happiness is also the fulfillment of our wants. This has nothing to do with satisfying our needs. It simply says: "I love myself." It is a gift of solitude we bring to our self by allowing peace to enter.

"Happiness is the absence of striving for happiness," affirms Chuang-tzu (369–286 B.C.). When we take an attitude of incompletion, a feeling of dissatisfaction, an action of striving or a stance of imperfection, we have created a process of seeking for something illusive rather than an achievement or attainment of a dream.

Swami Sachidananda of India said: "If you run after things, nothing will come to you. Let things run after you ... this is the secret of life."

Some say that a whole group of society must create happiness. I say, from personal experience, that we find happiness not only through connecting with others, but also through solitude. We can be happy being alone, simply enjoying the warmth of the sun, smelling the sea-scented breezes, hearing the melodious song of a canary, inhaling the sweet fragrance of lilac blossoms, or savoring a bit of honey. Or we can enjoy a euphoric relaxing moment captured by simply closing our eyelids or taking a deep breath as we retire on a recliner in the quiet of our reading room.

Key # 112 - Alone or with someone, happiness is a deliberate choice—a discipline acquired by self-control.

We can achieve happiness when we practice self-management. But how do we practice self-management?

- Enjoy an uncomplicated life style. Keep it simple!
- Meditate or take a moment to go within.
- Cultivate constructive and practical thoughts. Monitor your daily thoughts.

Discipline Delivers Happiness

Many of us may have never really thought about the possibility of controlling our state of mind. We may believe this is a natural process that simply "comes to us."

By the same token, most of us wish to find our bliss and stay there. Most of us wish to avoid suffering.

Key # 113 - Permanent happiness is virtually impossible for most of us unless we are willing to commit ourselves to self-control and discipline monitored by self-awareness.

Establishing a regimen that works is the most important aspect in the developing of a habit that brings happiness and not suffering. We want to avoid suffering at all costs!

Suffering affects the mental, emotional and physical systems. Witness the deterioration of a body when mental and emotional suffering have depleted it. The consequences are too familiar: weakness, dysfunction, serious illnesses and often premature death.

With the simple discipline of a daily meditation program, we can attain peace in our hearts. Through meditation we can simply and easily attain joy and expanded awareness.

For centuries, many cultures, including the Japanese, Hindus and American Indians, have recognized the value of meditation as a method for achieving health and happiness.

In a three-month stress measurement study conducted by West Virginia University-Morgantown, Kimberly A. Williams, Ph.D. reported that 62 "stressed out" subjects that made no changes in their routines other than adding meditation and yoga (disciplined thinking and a peaceful activity), showed improved health and reduction in stress symptoms. During that time, the subjects of the study made no other changes in their routines. They merely added disciplined thinking and a peaceful activity.

Writes Dr. Harold Bloomfield M.D., a practicing psychiatrist and director of psychiatry, psychotherapy and health at North County Holistic Health Center in Del Mar, California: "Inner silence has a profound effect on both body and mind." Dr. Bloomfield states that it raises resistance to diseases, increases mental clarity, heightens emotional ease and decreases blood pressure. Simply put, it restores vitality and opens the gate to happiness.

The mind–body link is strong and apparent. The life-force—the electromagnetic energy of the physical universe—supplies this connection. We truly are magical!

Laotze, in 500 B.C., said: "Dare to assert the I. Power is within ..." It is the force of this electromagnetic energy within us—inner silence, that creates wealth, relationships, health—and anything we desire. We must become cognizant of the great power within and take control of this energy in order to use it for our healing and our happiness.

Jesus said: "The Father that dwelleth in me, He doeth the works." (John 14:10)

Appropriate the power by first accepting that the power exists. You cannot appropriate it if you do not know it exists. You can only come to "know" through the power within.

"D" Stands for Destruction

Key # 114 - Attitudes of Disdain, Disappointment, Dissatisfaction and Delusion are poison to the sense of happiness and destructive to discipline.

Engaging in any activity that endangers growth within and blocks us to achieving happiness and autonomy, is toxic. Much suffering can be avoided if we retire to our inner self for our answers, and trust that we know what is best.

Turn Off the Outside World

I recommend the use of a mantra to begin a discipline; but never allow anything to become such a habit that it takes over your freedom to allow change to be constant. By consciously working in harmony with the universal power that enters our physical bodies through what has been long been called "the bridge"—the medulla oblongata in our brain—this life force brings the power of will into our beings. The practice of taking "time out" from the busy world and quieting the mind brings harmony between our outer and inner self.

Our electromagnetic energy physically and mentally gives us the ability to:

- work without fatigue.
- harness memory.
- accomplish a task quickly.
- have greater recall.
- have greater perseverance.

A Diseased Ego

Key # 115 - Suffering is an illness of the ego.

It literally "alters" the state of the ego. That is why it is called an alter-ego. You may have already noticed that when you retire to solitude and harmonize with your divine spark or inner self, you are untouched by suffering. In this quiet inner state, you make room for self-worth and re-form the alter-ego.

Key # 116 - Experiences of anguish cause an "altered" ego.

The more a person identifies with the human body and a specific pain, the more intense the torment will become. In a state of pure consciousness (detachment from the mindfulness of the physical body) there is only contentment. Disease and suffering do not exist.

The disharmony that exists in the world, the discord that causes one to suffer pain in some way, are nothing more than the illness of the ego, and misalignment with the physical body.

We can release this suffering by drawing energy from the inner silence accessed through discipline.

Inspiration Is the Child of Imagination

Key # 117 - Images are the keys to the invisible world.

Promptings, subtle vibrations of our electromagnetic energy assume the forms of distinct mental images. These, in turn, impel one to create something uplifting and of permanent value to humanity.

Inspiration comes through what you might call the transmission of super-consciousness (unlimited potential) into the subconscious (focused possibility). Discipline is a tool for acquiring undreamed-of possibilities.

When you think, you are using your mental or reasoning abilities of the brain. When you imagine, you awaken your vision. This activity, the bringing together of mental images and new ideas, affects every cell in our body, creating what I call a "joygasm."

Key #118 - *We visualize with our entire being.*

The ability to create, produce and manipulate mental images is called visualization—the art of imagination with passion. To visualize something is to create an idea in the mind and initiate its materialization. Since it is a well-known fact that form follows the idea, the power lies in capturing a desired idea.

It takes discipline to still the mind long enough to awaken the vision that will inspire us. Imagination is our shortest route to happiness.

I told you it was easy and magical!

How do you weigh your heart against a feather and have it balance? Imagination! Johannes Brahms, the great composer, said: "All true inspiration emanates from God, and He can reveal Himself to us only through that spark of divinity within— through what modern psychologists call subconscious mind."

What Do You Really Want?

Key # 119 - *Visualization gives energy to your dream.*

It propels it into the direction of a physical creation. However, you must remember to involve your emotional nature—your passion, for it to materialize. The degree of your passion and sense of trust in your dream will determine its materialization. You will not even need to twitch your nose or snap your head. Just passionately concentrate on what you want. Want is the key! Remember? "Be ye as a little child . . ."

When you produce images in your mind, you are in command of the release of electromagnetic energy. When you ignite an idea with energy, your body begins the production of hormones, which are the building blocks to the materialization of your want. By focused imagination you create images in your frontal lobe (the quiet area of your brain that occupies forty percent of the neo-cortex). This singularity of attention brings about your dream. The neo-cortex acts like the architect. It is the area of our brain responsible for constructing holographic images around which the idea forms. Once the dream is fully formed it is transferred to the frontal lobe, where the magic begins.

Each internal energy state has corresponding mental imagery. The chemical messages that are carried in our hormones will deliver the codes necessary for the manifestation of the dream. You will be surprised at the power of your own creative force. By evoking the proper imagery through visualization, without restrictions upon your desires, you can bring about your much wanted state of bliss.

The chemistry of billions of cells throughout your body, especially those in your body's central nervous system, will change in response to what you imagine. This is the reason for dreaming with passion. It is also the reason for giving no energy whatsoever to anything you do not wish to experience!

Five Basic Steps to Developing a Powerful Imagination

1. Set your dream clearly in your frontable lobe—your movie screen.
Often we do not know what our desires really are. You can determine where your wants may be by listing

them. Check your response to each by asking yourself how you feel about them. Does this one make your heart race? Do you feel a flutter of excitement? Anticipation? Number your desires in the order of preference. Which dream do you want to achieve first? Second?

Enjoy the journey. Learn to allow the natural development of an idea. Disregard anything that you might call impatience. The dwelling on any notions of frustration will cancel the dream and cause your frustration to accelerate. Work on your most immediate selections first. Get used to your dream idea. When you allow yourself to imagine, you bring the dream into focus. Bringing productive imagination to the forefront is the key here—to see and feel your idea as an actuality. This desire is on its way to becoming the dream in the physical.

2. Assist in the creation of the image by using sensual aids.

The use of pictures you have taken of something close to the idea you are visualizing: cut-outs from magazines that resemble what you are desiring, the scent of perfume or cologne, the feel of satin or leather, the taste of chocolate; will serve as stimulants in your mind for what you want. A beach with a sunset, a waterfall in the distant tropical foliage, a ski slope with glistening snow, support your dream. Why do you think advertising with images works so well?

Remember: Thinking is not imagery. Thinking is reasoning, after you have created the mental image (imagination = image-in-motion). By use of your five senses you will determine exactly what you wish to create; such as, the color of your car, the great smell of its soft leather interior; the smooth sound of a new engine. Pictures help you with your ideas.

The senses need to take part in the image you are creating. Thinking creates the details of the idea, giving it physical reality through the senses. Describe and enrich the experience with your own written comments on these visuals. Apply to your visualization a clearly stated decree. Explicit words add to the intensity of your passion.

Be specific and discriminating with the words you choose to describe your desire. Depict exactly what and how you desire your dream to be realized ... for example, its name, color, weight, height, texture, scent, etc.

To give you an example of what happens when you do not declare specifically what you desire, here is one of my own recent experiences:

I made a note on my calendar: "Sign a new lease." I was not specific enough, because when it came to the date, I found myself in a situation in which the landlord wanted to move back into her home and would not renew my lease. I found myself signing a new lease all right, but it was for a different home! Not being specific enough on my part caused the energy of the other person's more specific idea to come into play. The physically exhausting move was not what I had in mind. But I did "sign a new lease."

3. Focus often on your desire.

At least three times a day focus upon your specific desire. Take yourself mentally to that place. It is necessary to do your conscious focusing as often as possible through the course of the day. Look at the pictures you have used and read the words you have written. Concentrate totally on that dream. Imagining is the discipline it takes to create specifics. By constant practice and meditation, the mental atmosphere forms around the imagined details of your desire. The rest is just a matter of time.

Address one dream at a time. This will allow you to be more forceful in projecting the energy into one directed idea. The power is within you to give your wish the energy to become a reality.

Create that relationship with the special someone that you have dreamed of for so long! Impatience is a form of control sourced from insecurity. Impatience shows a lack of trust.

Happiness is a choice brought about by our own imagination.

4. Give your idea a positive future.

Remember that trusting yourself and believing in your desires initiates a magical force that will permeate the universe. Let the ship (your dream) take off and return with its treasure.

"Imagery" is the captain of a ship. It controls the outcome or your destiny. Allowing the idea to reach its destination can be compared to the trust of sailors for their captain.

Imagination is the magical power that travels through space attracting the energy that it needs in order to become a physical and concrete reality.

Your statement of words—your decree, is the power to direct material changes.

Imagination is an ancient universal power all of us can access. And with it, we can engender the pattern around which the visualized mental image forms itself. As soon as we have voiced those creative words into the atmosphere, we have ignited the ethereal image. Once we have worked out a formula of words according to our desires, these words will illicit concreteness.

It is not merely holding a focus that causes the desire to manifest. In order to initiate the action, we must also endow the formula we have created with our decree.

Releasing our words in a forceful manner by voicing them into the ethers establishes the power of the imagination, the power of manifestation. This is why children, who do this as a matter of habit, get what they persistently ask for. They enforce it with the power of the word.

By this process you create the image into the exact idea that you have originated by your thoughts and supported with your words. Own your dream; assert it. Know it will happen; project it. "Don't worry; be happy."

5. Wait patiently for its realization.

"How can I do that?" you will ask. Just do it, and witness the results. You will then need no further proof. You must maintain totally creative attention in the birth of this desire as you calmly await the realization of your idea. Now you must give it force by maintaining the idea fresh in your mind with all of the internal energy you can possibly muster. It will become your reality!

Then, do everything that is in your power to make the idea come true. You might be tempted to ask: "What about the money it takes to pay for the materialization of this idea?" Be assured that if you do all that is in your power (in happiness) to honestly bring about the necessary means, it will be there—just like magic.

Know it!!!

Don't count the minutes. Do not doubt; have no fear. Know it! Fear destroys creative energy and your dream will suffer its effects. Fear is also an alternative creative energy which in turn will materialize the very thing you fear. The strong, clear and defined mental image is the framework around which the actual material conditions form themselves. Like magic it all begins to happen.

After you have mastered these steps you will experience the happiness of your dreams come true.

Allowing the universal forces to do their bidding is the greatest discipline you can live.

Discipline Is a Spiritual Requirement

Key # 120 - A spirited person is not controlling of others but demonstrates discipline and self-control.

A spirited person thinks "can" instead of "can't." By cultivating an attitude of determination, high courage and modesty, you do not have to prove anything by words or actions. When you hold your head up high, indicating you have walked through the valleys and also climbed high and challenging mountains, you show the world that you are disciplined.

You feel disciplined. When you have smelled the roses and also have been pricked by their thorns, you have earned the mark of a warrior. Discipline never takes anything away from you; in fact, it causes you to gain something more—your inner strength. Oria Mountain Dreamer, an Indian Elder said in a poem called "The Invitation": "It doesn't interest me how old you are, I want to know if you will risk looking like a fool for love, for your dream, for the adventure of being alive."

From now on, you will seldom have a dismal day because you know what happiness is all about. In your journey you have earned it. You have traveled through life, all the while gaining spiritual strength in spite of stumbling-blocks along the way. Your experiences have served you; they have allowed you to become well aware of who and what you are. You are where you are today as a result of yesterday's thoughts, words and actions. You are a masterpiece, created by every step you have taken!

Key # 121 - Use past experiences as stepping-stones to new heights.

These experiences provide insight. They are the guidebook each of us develops. Most of us have had a surplus of experiences that at the time may have not seemed to offer much advice for the future. A divorce, bankruptcy or other business failure, rejection from a social group, failure to win a contest or competition, may seem at the time like experiences we'd like to bury with a hatchet. As we grow and analyze these experiences, we realize they are not stumbling but building blocks. They have allowed us to move onward and upward, beyond their momentary disappointment or feelings of shame and failure.

These experiences are your children. As their parent, would you disown them, disown yourself just because you fell off your bike the first few times you tried to ride it? Or fell down a few times when you were trying to learn how to walk without holding onto anything?

Self-Trust Delivers Happiness

Most of us want fast answers. Quick fixes. We do not want to do the work involved in getting from A to B.

How many people do you know who are chronic complainers only looking for ears that will hear their diatribes against the unfairness of life? These people are not looking for a solution. They are refusing to claim the very thing they are struggling to attain.

They are getting in their own way.

Their thoughts are literally writing the book of their own lives. Their actions are screaming out in bold headlines the title of their autobiography: LIFE IS UNFAIR. I'LL NEVER GET WHAT I WANT. NO ONE REALLY CARES ABOUT ME. I WAS BORN TO BE A FAILURE. I ALWAYS GET THE BAD BREAKS. And so on. You can probably fill in hundreds of similar titles because you've heard so many of these litanies before from friends and family. Maybe you've even heard them from yourself, before you picked up this book!

Key #122 - When we choose the key called trust, we can open the door to contentment.

We will not need to calculate or determine outcomes. We can be assured that when we trust that we will indeed achieve the outcomes we desire, we will get results. We will produce the happiness we're looking for.

Shirley came to me on a weekly basis to get her hair done; this weekly ritual was important to her. When she was a teenager, Shirley had lost her right arm in a boat accident. This may have closed one world to her, but it opened up another. Shirley was talkative and expressive. She often told me about her involvement in theater performances when she was in high school and how this gave her a sense of worth.

Shirley's grandfather was her teacher and life coach. It was he who had suggested that she get involved in something she really enjoyed doing, where she could shine. He knew if Shirley were to focus on her talents, her inner worth rather than her physical or outer appearance, she would develop confidence and strong feelings of self-worth.

One can appreciate that the loss of an arm at any age produces a feeling of shame and inferiority; to a teenager, dependent on peer pressure for self-worth, it would be devastating.

Shirley followed her grandfather's advice and soon discovered that life was really not much different from taking a part in a play. With tears in her eyes, she shared with me her discovery of a great and beautiful power within. She found how her inner happiness projected outward in her relationships with others.

Shirley gave me one of the best examples I could have possibly asked for, of the power of self-discipline and its ability to turn on one's inner light. It is that light that causes people to love and admire you. It is that light that is the source of our happiness.

Shirley learned to trust herself by letting go of her fears.

When you have come to understand yourself better through discipline, you will discover that you are more flexible and open to new experiences. As you develop self-control and self-tracking skills, you will not be surprised to find life full of excitement and rich opportunities. You will hum inside. Your life will be in harmony with self-love. You will feel the warmth of nature's rhythm and truly enjoy your self. Some people call this "being in the flow."

Buy Your Fears a One-Way Ticket

My client Connie has a special method for dealing with her fears. "I always begin my day with a deep meditation," she told me when she first started coming for haircuts. "I spend most of that time going through the day and planning it. I want to be sure that I'm armed and ready for all the possibilities of things that could go wrong. I want to make sure I can handle all my fears."

"So how is that working for you?" I asked.

"Actually," she admitted, "it only makes me more frightened about taking risks or making changes in my life ... even when I know I need to make those changes in order to get where I want to go. Jeanette, I'm really a very frightened person, and I don't know what to do about it! I start to play those 'what if' games with myself, and pretty soon I'm terrified about all the horrible things that could happen to me. Just walking out the front door becomes a challenge!"

I suggested that Connie start practicing a disciplined rather than undisciplined meditation. By using the steps outlined in this book, Connie learned how to access her subconscious mind and reach the still point inside. By creating a sacred space rather than "scared" disorganized clutter, she gave her self room to grow and focus on its worth. The experience became a positive productive one.

It didn't take long for Connie to dispel the fears and start moving forward with freedom and confidence. She still practices disciplined meditation every morning.

Brian is another person who came to realize he was his own worst enemy. His fearful doubting thoughts created an aura of skepticism. Brian had a habit of not speaking his truth but only re-iterating to others what he thought they wanted to hear.

The tracking exercises in this book worked wonders for Brian. He started to work on self-awareness and discovered that by evaluating his thoughts and speaking his truth, he was able to bring more harmony and happiness into his life.

Angela, a delightful little bit of a girl, came into my shop one day many years ago to get a permanent. We had a couple of hours of intense conversation about the fears that were chiseling away at her self-worth. "Man, I'm really letting myself down," she sighed as I unrolled the perm rods off her hair.

"Sort of like what I'm doing here with your hair," I said jokingly.

"I haven't been loving myself enough to understand and release my fears," she continued. "I'm going to make more changes than just my hairdo," she whispered under her breath.

"Your hair looks great!" I chirped, scrunching it one more time with a towel. As we fixed it into the "new do," both Angela and her hair shone. She had awakened to the need to adjust her value of self-love and had begun this "change" by giving personal pampering a priority.

From that time on, she scheduled a monthly trip to the beauty shop, and soon her fears began to vanish.

"My wife tells me you have a way with people," said Russ as he seated himself in the styling chair.

"What exactly are you referring to?" I inquired.

"Oh, Ingrid told me that you gave her some insight on some stuff she had been struggling with for months. When she got to thinking about it, your words made sense and she changed her outlook in a New York second. That's some kind of magic, if you ask me!" he declared.

"Oh Russ," I exclaimed, pumping up the hydraulic chair to position it at the proper height and eyeing him in the mirror, "the real truth is that she wanted you to come in for a good haircut and she got the best of you!"

"No, I've seen the change in her," he insisted. "What really freaks me out is that now I've become different too."

"Really?"

"I think you have some secrets I need to figure out. How can I be sure that I'm always the winner?"

"That's an easy one, Russ," I replied. "You just need to only make sure you're not in competition with anyone because of some hidden fear, a little voice inside that's nagging you and telling you you're not going to win after all. That competition includes yourself. Then you'll have no problem about winning."

Russ was silent for a moment. "Sounds easy enough." he said at length. "Now about my haircut ..."

The Many Faces of Fear

In our life's journey we have become sensitive to our emotions or feelings about our situation. These emotions, as we've said, are created by our thought process. They are the body's chemical reactive outcomes or responses communicated through our brain's neural-net pathways.

Key # 123 - Emotions are the effect of an experience rather than its cause or origin.

This is why it is so easy to detect emotions, once you know what they feel and look like.

For example, when you were a child you may have had the experience of running down a river bank on a path made slippery by fallen leaves. If you fell down, twisting your ankle, this memory may cause you to experience fear whenever you confront a steep bank thereafter. This emotion is a memory. In order for you to enjoy running down that hill, you will need a fresh experience in which you do not fall and hurt yourself.

The trick is to become sensitive enough to these emotional reactive modes. Then, switch those neural pathways to new and improved neurological connections. I know at first it is very difficult to engage this type of thinking. The "wormholes" are more real than you might think. Spooky? Try it and hang in there; you will enjoy the improved outcome!

Our conscious mind tends to get stuck on the past. Dutifully the brain serves its purpose of imprinting memory. It isn't that fear has a tendency for anything; it's the conscious mind (neo-cortex) that has a tendency to rationalize, or find a reason for things, in order to be "right." The conscious mind makes a habit of disguising fear as denial, self-blame, avoidance, blaming others, and jest or joking.

The rational mind can trigger an unlimited chain of future possibilities to be afraid of or to worry about, losing rationality in the process. When our security centers are rattled by constant fear, worry, anxiety or despair we become numb to our subconscious mind—our sense of natural insight. Disappointment, frustration and boredom are merely the numbing of our sensory organs by our own refusal to give up the past.

Key #124 - *When we experience a fear we trigger a passion and cause a memorable imprint.*

If we repeatedly experience an enjoyable sensation, we tend to become satiated and bore ourselves. The brain is a powerful recording instrument. Disappointment, boredom and frustration are signs of the constant nagging fear of loss and the repetitive letdown after momentarily enjoyable sensations. If these are allowed to continue they mature into anger, resentment, irritation, hostility and hate. Eventually they start to destroy our power-seeking stimulations.

If it is anger, resentment, irritation, hostility and hate that cause us to passionately imprint a memory, then we continually defend and try to control others and situations we feel are out of our power to control. These escalating emotional responses are the downward spiral of our self-worth. They are the cause of mental, physical and emotional illnesses and dysfunction.

Fear becomes our comfort zone. It provides the illusion of security because it is a familiar feeling. We have experienced it before. Fear of the unknown—constructive feelings of hope, confidence, trust and self-love are far more frightening.

The emotions of fear, worry and anxiety become associated with our feelings of security. If these are threatened by the mind's ability to trigger an unlimited chain of future possibilities, or "what if's," to worry about, we endanger our self-control as well as our self-worth.

Key #125 - Anger is a false sense of power, another type of fear that elicits subtle control of others.

Anger is an emotion highly charged with chemicals produced by the endocrine system of the human body. It is a chemical memory that continues to run through the neural connections already blazed and it continues to disintegrate self-love, self-worth and self-control. It is relentless when it comes to relationships because it has no respect for the outcome. It only seeks to be expressed.

My daughter Raquel shared with me one of her great discoveries of how she overcame certain fears that she was confronting. She'd been involved with civil court matters while attempting to come to an agreement with her husband after a separation. Raquel came to realize that when she released her anger expressed through arrogance and pride and started to live a more disciplined self-observant life, she opened herself to gladness—and gratitude.

Her frustrations concerning the court matter were resolved without stress and contention. She came to understand that a loving and caring attitude was more fruitful than anger.

Raquel had won her own fight; she had come to bear her truth. She took a more understanding posture with unconditional love toward herself and others. She studded her crown with another gem—happiness through disciplined self-worth.

Key # 126 - "Selfless service" is another form of fear.

We can become so involved in helping others, we neglect ourselves. This type of service is rooted in the need for approval and the fear of not being accepted.

Fear can disguise itself as denial and bring about much unhappiness. Sandra is an example. One early summer morning, she came bouncing into my shop, bright and cheerful as usual. Or so I thought.

"Jeanette," she declared as soon as she had settled into the styling chair, "my face is smiling, but my heart is heavy with regrets and denial."

"Why so? I asked. "It's very unusual for you to be unhappy."

A shadow crossed over her face. "I wasn't really honest when I told my brother that I didn't care if he didn't have a job, and that he could come to live with me."

I looked her in the eye, "You didn't mean that?"

"No, I want him to have a job and I can't afford to have him live with me. I really wasn't being honest with myself."

"Then call him back and tell him how you really feel," I advised her.

"I'm confused," Sandra shook her head. "I guess I never got over the hate I had for him. I keep denying this and have never settled it with him."

"This will continue to bother you until you talk with him and tell him the truth." I gave her a tissue and the hairstyle book.

Sandra handed me back the book and stood up. "You're right. I can't wait another minute. I have to do that right now. I have to get it off my chest. I'll be back this afternoon for my haircut."

"You'll feel better later, I guarantee it," I exclaimed, giving her a hug. "Later we'll select a new haircut for you!"

Empower Yourself

I'm sure you have often heard the statement: "No one makes you angry." What you may not hear more than once or twice perhaps—if ever, is: "No one makes you do anything."

Key #127 - You are solely responsible for everything that you feel.

Often it is not easy to take, or accept responsibility for our own feelings—"our own creations." Often we use anger and worry as defense mechanisms because they are memory imprints sourced from past emotions. These emotions in turn are linked to experiences we would prefer to forget. But because they are deeply embedded in the unconscious they do not seem to go away. That is, unless we allow ourselves to temporarily turn off our conscious mind and access these imprints. As I have suggested previously, meditation is one of the best ways to release these unwanted programs or imprints.

Key # 128 - Much of anger and worry are based on labeling.
We tend to blame ourselves for things we label as "bad."

Emil is an example of self-blame. A handsome young man who seemed to be "an accident waiting to happen," Emil came in regularly for haircuts. His body had gone through innumerable painful accidents. At one time he came in with one of his arms in a sling.

"Got pushed over in the skating rink," he told me.

Another time he came in with his foot in a cast. "Got my big toe accidentally chopped off at my construction job," he explained, struggling to find a comfortable way to sit in the chair.

"Dropped an anvil on my toe and totally demolished it. The other guy walked right in front of me."

"Interesting!" was all I could say to keep from getting taken in by his drama. Emil was hurting himself. He felt "victim" to circumstances beyond his control. "Read some of Louise Hay's books," I suggested, "She shows you how you can heal your life. In fact, that's one of her best-known books."

As soon as Eric started to take a detached view of himself and make the changes necessary to bring happiness and self-love into his life, he saw a totally different picture. Emil began a slow but tedious study of his own emotions.

"I found peace within myself," he reported happily when he came in for his next haircut. "My life started to change after I stopped blaming others and myself."

Frances was a shy yet inquisitive girl in her twenties. She came to see me for her haircuts every month and shared many personal feelings with me in conversation.

"I don't have a lot of friends," she confessed, "but I would like to have many."

I was curious about her statement and asked, "Why do you suppose that is?"

"I can never find anybody to really be friends with," she answered.

"Where do you spend most of your time?" I asked her.

"Well, I guess I like to go to the library and read." Frances said shyly.

"Wow! I suppose you can talk to lots of people there," I joked.

"I guess not," she agreed.

"Lots of characters in those books, but no friends to play with, huh?" I quipped.

"Yeah, I guess I've sort of avoided people," Frances admitted.

"A new hair do will get you going in a new direction!" I declared, walking with her to the shampoo bowl. "Try the park or the bookstore."

"I will!" Frances promised.

"They say the grocery store is good too," I told her as she slipped out the door.

Frances found her friends. Everywhere. And she still had her friends in the books that she loved to read. In fact, she even found many friends who, like herself, loved to read. They planned library and lunch excursions together.

Clara, unlike Frances, is bold and direct.

"What are you going to give me today, a shear experience?" she joked, plunking herself down in my styling chair.

"All right, young one. I'll 'sheer' those locks off you today!" I declared, taking her up on her pun.

Clara started to vent. "Man, the last time I was nice to someone they just turned around and bit me where it hurts. That's the last time I'll do something for him!"

"Watch out." I warned. "You're liable to get pulled in on their drama."

"What are you talking about?" Clara eyed me darkly.

"I'm just wondering if you have any idea how you bring yourself to these situations by allowing the wind to push you to and fro."

"I'm doing what?" Clara leafed through a hairstyling book.

"You might be getting pulled into someone else's drama," I repeated. "Check it out."

When Clara came to see me the next time, I found a welcome change in her attitude of blaming.

"I'm another gal today!" she proudly chirped.

"You can sure tell that right away," I encouraged. Clara then proceeded to relate to me how she had started to turn around her life by taking responsibility for her actions.

"I really do feel different," she admitted. "I feel like I've got myself in charge of my self!"

"Exactly," I beamed, giving her a hug.

Key #129 - Forgiveness comes much more easily when you begin to realize that no one really "did it" to you.

There is no real satisfaction or redemption in revenge. Forgive and lighten your burdens. Your entire being will be bathed in the tranquility of a feather-light heart. When you understand and accept that you are a part of the great Universal Mind and that everything has a grand design in the "bigger picture," you will come to live in peace and happiness, your heart balanced evenly against a feather.

Shame Comes Packed with Emotions

Why does shame have such a strong hold on us?

Key # 130 - As children we receive messages from adults that cause us to imprint emotions in our memory banks with messages of shame and guilt.

At that age we haven't yet learned how to deal with these messages in order to release their destructive imprint.

We tend to forget that parents do the best they can. They are also dealing with memory patterns, programs or imprints. Often they too have not yet learned how to release burdensome ones. Thus, these emotional imprints are transmitted from one generation to the next through genetics, language, behavior, and attitude. Parents treat their children just as they were treated.

Internalizing shame by remaining in the destructive patterns after having recognized them, deteriorates self worth. Imprinting shame in deep levels of consciousness tears the fabric of self-worth.

How do we release this shame? How do we break these destructive patterns? Commitment to a discipline such as meditation, yoga or focused relaxation is one of the best ways to overcome feelings of worthlessness.

Key #131 - Acquire a thirst for knowledge.

Establish a habit of seeking out inspirational, informative, motivational books, cassette tapes or CDs to read and listen to. Attend retreats and seminars. All of these activities are ways to grow and change these unwanted patterns.

Key # 132 - Shame not only destroys the sense of trust in self; it also has an uncanny ability to debilitate one's intuitiveness.

Shame leads to the questioning of our feelings and perceptions. These are our most basic and natural barometer about ourselves, others, and our environment.

Dr. Harold Bloomfield, M.D. cites the healing power of inner silence as a way of healing the psyche ". . . without having to verbalize or examine long-buried emotional trauma."

Trust Intuition—Dispel Self-Blame

Key # 133 - Dare to trust your intuition for resolving issues.

Take risks. Start by forgiving yourself and suspending the feeling of blame. Self-blame comes in many disguises. It shows you your past as a re-run of mistakes. It turns up sadness, resentment, regret, remorse and many other chemically charged, unwanted emotions.

The medicine for happiness is allowing the past to be released and forgiven by trusting your intuition. This requires self-love. Dare to love yourself.

Dare to ask yourself for joy, and it will be yours. Unwanted emotions connected to self-blame will vanish.

Key # 134 - Once you place the cornerstone of integrity— integration or wholeness, getting it all together—in the base of electromagnetic energy around your auric field, you have begun to build your castle of nobility.

Your spirit and mind have accomplished the foundation that tells others you have reached your zenith of bliss. Others will be able to sense your exuberance and zest for life; they will note your inner core of truth. You will have come to a place in your life where your word is truth and your demeanor will soothe others; you will be known as a charismatic individual. Your contribution to the world will be a compassionate heart and a helping hand.

Key # 135 - As long as you remain trusting with an open mind about life, you will sail freely and have control over your destiny.

You will have harnessed the magical power of love, and self worth. I knew I had turned a new page and earned another gem for my crown of attitudes when I was able to give unconditional love to myself and everyone alike. No longer did I give up my dream of happiness for the myriad of distractions such as other people's dramas, and my lack of knowledge.

I now remained true to myself, stable and unbending. This change has delivered the happiness I sought.

It has also defined for me the true meaning of unconditional love, and how to acquire it:

1. Through consciousness of what I am doing and why I am doing it,

2. A decision to make the necessary changes, and
3. A disciplined program of action.

If you find that your creative spark is weak, use the following ideas for firing-up the engine. Soon you will start to feel those creative juices flowing again:

1. If you feel moody, toss aside that mood and keep moving forward.
2. Sometimes things begin to seem too tough for comfort. Just put them on hold and take a vacation (in your own town if necessary; but get away from home!).
3. Difficult moments are normal for everyone. They too shall pass and you will discover they were mostly illusionary.
4. Keep your chin up and stop doubting yourself.
5. Face the "mean monster" and make it work for you instead. What could be so fatal? Proceed without hesitation.
6. Check out your surroundings. Are you associating with self-destructive people? Keep company with creative people who support your ideals.
7. Take charge of your responsibilities and do not regret any move you make.
8. Become accountable for your own thinking and become more creative with your imagination.
9. Control freaks are everywhere; don't be counted among them. There is such a thing as destructive control.
10. Stop trying to figure out what you really want; just start living as if you already have it.
11. Have a party! Celebrate your life; pat yourself on the back and congratulate yourself.
12. Become a "floaty" for a day; or do the "coasting" game for a few days. Watch how magical things start to happen.

Tracking Question

1. How would you describe imagination?
2. What seems to be in the way of your happiness?
3. What two fears are the most vivid in your mind?
4. Has shame caused you to stop trusting yourself? Why? Why not?
5. How would you describe the electromagnetic energy around your aura?
6. Would you consider yourself a controlling person? Why? Why not?

Tracking Exercises

1. In your journal, list five people you are willing to release as you forgive yourself for things you still remember. As you go down the list, make a small note of your anger issues toward each person, or your feelings of hate toward them. For example: My friend Frank running over my dog with his truck.

    The purpose of this exercise is to get in touch with those feelings of anger, resentment, hatred and blame that you may be harboring. Allow yourself to fully feel these emotions. Write a small statement about the sensations that are re-lived within your body; the way you feel about the "re-run" of the experience. Understand that these are chemically induced messages electrically fired up by the thoughts you have captured emotionally in your focused attention. Relax; this exercise is to allow you to feel, to become aware and to understand the mechanisms that you live with. You are learning to be in control of these feelings and not enslaved by them. These are only memories and illusions of what you once felt. You are recalling them to recognize how powerful they are in your life. Let them go. Promise yourself not to allow this bio-chemically electromagnetic charged memory to trigger emotion again.

2. Now, using the same list, next to their name and the feeling you have written, list what you are willing to receive in exchange for your self-forgiveness. As you create space for your greater good in forgiving, you will also bring into your life a "treasure." For example: Kris didn't pay me back the $50 dollars I lent him. "I am willing to receive help from others for having helped him."

3. The word is very powerful. This part of the exercise is for you to voice your statement. Next, forgive the person on your list for everything, carefully going through each item listed. For example: "I forgive you, Mike, for the dent you put in my car." The purpose here is to recognize your judgmental and emotional involvement and to rejoice in having lived through the experience. Love these people for having played the script you gave them in your drama. It was all in divine order!

4. Taking the same list of names, now write a message of love toward them for having taken part in your journey of life. Active imagination is the key.

5. List three dreams you wish to manifest that will bring great happiness to you. Keep a running diary of how they come to materialize themselves.

6. Create your own instruction manual for happiness.

Chapter 8

Humor: A Tool to Self Fulfillment

"Humor ... the ability to create unlimited perceptions so that we can deal with the ups and downs of life, and have fun doing it."

— Jim Keelan

Most of us would agree that people rarely succeed at anything unless they have fun doing it. A sense of humor—being able to perceive something as funny and deriving pleasure from the way it "tickles your funny bone" adds even more to the experience.

Key # 136 - Laughter allows you to release tension from your physical body.

It helps you relax and brings a sense of fulfillment to the entire system. Experiments have shown a strong positive connection between a sense of humor and a healthy attitude. It has been proven that laughter raises oxygen levels in the blood by increasing your respiration as a result of the acceleration of your heart rate. Humor is also an avenue to passion. Since animals do not experience humor, you can count on it being a very special human trait that has a touch of the divine. Consider the similarity of the words "humor" and "human." Does that tell us something, also?

Key # 137 - Joy is not brought to you by another; you bring joy to yourself.

Happiness—the genuine "sense of humor," is a feeling of joy. Your ability to cope with frustrating moments is largely increased by an optimistic attitude. Optimism is one of the by-products of a sense of humor. When you laugh at a situation, you shift your point of view. This causes you to give yourself a moment to re-arrange your emotions.

Humor occurs from your visualization of a series of fast-shifting images often accompanied by participation of the other senses as well. You'll tend to giggle or laugh outright. This laughter increases your ability to breathe better and your heart works with less stress. Remember, breath is your source of life and your heart is the pump that keeps the blood flowing through your veins.

Humor can also be that sudden unexpected understanding that tickles your inner composure. The feeling that overtakes you is the result of something you did not anticipate that occurs after a moment of awareness. This is due to the contrast in images: what you would ordinarily expect that is supplanted by another picture. The ensuing laughter is the elixir of a pleasing appreciation for life.

The value of humor lies in "living happily with yourself." Sometimes things are funnier if you can see yourself in a situation that you are currently dealing with. When you can do this from a distance, you gain the courage to proceed through otherwise challenging circumstances. This is why humor has been known to be the key to adapting oneself to sometimes difficult obstacles. It allows us to adjust matters to the peculiarities or exigencies of life's unusual predicaments.

The family name for my children is Peil. When Danna, my second daughter, was growing up, on the playground, children used to taunt her and make fun of her name, "Danna Peil," because of its similarity to Banana Peel. They would chant, "Danna Banana, Danna Banana Peel!"

Danna became the subject of cruel play for children in the playground, but instead of feeling victimized, she took their taunts with a sense of humor and shouted back: "Yes, I am a Peil! But what you guys don't know is that us Peil girls have that great Peil appeal!"

Danna used humor as a tool to lighten up the situation. This allowed her to let her classmates' cruel insults roll off her back. A sense of humor gave her the tool for shifting her point of view and calling on her creativity. Quickly and easily she found a way to have fun with a situation that could have been devastating for a sensitive child at an age when acceptance by her peers is critical.

Of all my six daughters, Danna is the only one who chose to keep Peil as her last name after she was married!

Humor Is the Oil in the Engine of Your Experiences

Key # 138 - One of the requirements of self-fulfillment is the ability to gracefully make fun of yourself and feel good about it.

Give priority to the development of a playful attitude toward yourself. Fear of appearing foolish often overshadows the ability to have fun and love yourself.

Probably you recall a time in the past when you were laughing and being foolish—"just for the fun of it," and someone reprimanded you, telling you to "grow up." This programming has caused many of us to develop a fear about appearing foolish to others unless we act in "an acceptable way."

Too often we have been drilled to accept only certain behaviors. As a result, we may have developed robotic responses that we use as self-protection whenever we feel the need to "fit in."

In time we may discover that "looking foolish" is simply a matter of perception.

If you fear looking foolish to others, examine yourself first. Perhaps you have a transparent belief that says "I will be disrespectful of others if I laugh, or make fun." Perhaps you are attached to the need to be accepted, or receive approval. Do you often criticize others? Do you look at others as foolish when they express themselves in a manner that is different from your own? Do you have expectations of yourself?

Release the fear of appearing foolish to others and you will discover that a lovingly humorous attitude toward yourself first will be a firm foundation to your success in dealing with others.

As a tool to realized self-worth, humor says, "I love myself!" You reflect the way you feel about yourself to others. When you are in a good mood, you smile. I like to call humor the oil in the engine of your experiences. If you feel grumpy, you see yourself through the eyes of a grumpy person with low self-esteem and bruised self-worth. Aristotle once said: "All friendly feelings toward others come from the friendly feelings a person has for himself."

This clearly tells you that the oil in the engine is personal happiness. Happiness begins within yourself. How you perceive yourself will be reflected in the world of your experiences, in the way you relate to others and the pleasures you derive from your sense of good humor.

Laughter is Contagious

Key # 139 - Your friends are those who can laugh with and not at you.

You will notice that when you are around a group, your laugh is louder and more robust. You might even feel okay if you happened to wet your pants from laughing harder! We feel more secure, as though we have more freedom of expression when we are part of a group.

It is also important to recognize how you identify with the group; become aware of your own actions and re-actions as you express yourself. Be careful to choose associations with groups that support similar values. Choose to be in an environment of love and compassion. Laughing together is refreshing, healthy, and conducive to self-fulfillment.

Janis, one of the girls who works in my salon, has a knack for having fun and expressing her genuine good humor. Her laughter is contagious and refreshing to everyone in the salon.

Around 2 PM she starts in on her afternoon giggles; we often jest with her about the setting of the clock by her outburst of joy. Janis is perfect refreshment for the afternoon lulls. She laughs at the simplest things and brings joy to others around her with her delightful sense of humor.

Key # 140 - The ability to perceive a situation with humor gives you the power to evaluate it with strength.

Thus, you increase your creative skills and develop keener abilities. You walk through a situation with a smile and feeling of accomplishment.

Enthusiasm goes hand in hand with humor; it is also contagious. If you wish to evoke enthusiasm from others, be enthusiastic yourself. It works like a charm!

With a sense of humor, we augment our ability to cope with life's little quirks and seeming stumbling blocks. Your unique perceptions and creative responses to a situation by seeing it from the vantage of humor creates a new neural-net track for your emotions. This is a healthy path on which to travel.

When we can acquire a strong ability to perceive ourselves from an optimistic perspective, regardless of the seeming aspects of our physical appearance, our names, the sound of our voice, the way our unique expression is perceived by others or the way we "look" to someone else, we have tapped into the source of joy.

You have the power to recognize and capitalize on your own uniqueness. The magic you can create is sublime.

Develop a Playful Attitude toward Life

Key # 141 - Our responsibility lies in having a sense of humor with a profound respect for others.

Often we forget that each of us is distinctive in the way we express ourselves. We may get side-tracked and consider ourselves weird instead of unique and creative. Our uniqueness requires conscientious responsibility and enthusiastic determination to view life with a playful attitude.

Having a playful attitude is not a license to make fun of others, nor does it indicate a "better than thou" attitude. Humor is commonly known as "wit"—the ability to be happy and strong against stress.

Michelle, an intelligent and receptive girl in her late twenties, came to see me for her monthly hair cut and color one evening after work. From her tensed jaw and the pain in her expression, I knew she was highly stressed and dealing with an unresolved situation. I soon learned that her supervisor had been too direct and saber-tongued in their last meeting. "She doesn't have to go about it that way," said Michelle, almost in tears.

"What happened to your sense of humor?" I asked her.

"Man, she was so bad, I lost it! I wanted to cry."

"How are you going to get over this one?"

"The moment I caught myself in a 'victim' attitude, I remembered what you had told me some time ago about using my good humor—but I was too involved. Darn it! Next time I won't let myself become so sensitive." Ruefully she shook her head as her expression cleared and her eyes lightened.

"And ... always be prepared to forgive yourself for those times when you re-act to others' harshness," I added. "Let yourself become harmonious with your inner calm. Allow your passion for life to awaken within you. Then you can be your true humorous and happy self!"

Key # 142 - Life's vicissitudes can sometimes numb our senses.

Dulled senses lead to dulled perception and indifference. Passion, zest for life disappears. Often, levels of stress, or prolonged lethargy become so overwhelming, we may end up physically or emotionally ill.

How do we break free from the stresses of daily life? Often, we may not be aware that most of our stress is caused by our concern for others. Remember: it is not your job to bring joy to another; they must do that for themselves.

Take time to feel the world around you. Let your senses absorb the simple, often unnoticed things. Can you hear the waves lapping against the shore? The sweet hum of the motor boats and happy shouts of the water skiers? Hear the gurgle of almost any baby, anywhere, and see the twinkle in their eyes as they clap hands with you? Did you see the new blossoms on the tree above the dumpster where you empty your trash? Or feel the stiff hot desert wind brushing against your cheek, ruffling up your hair? Did you smell the sweetness of the air after rain? And what about this evening's sunset—the way those magnificent rose colors streak across the sky ... everywhere ... above elegant homes, city buildings, used car lots, scrap metal yards, impeccably kept gardens ...?

Did you watch the traffic come to a halt, the cars lining up like soldiers, while the mothers and fathers helped their children onto the school bus? Did you see how they smiled and waved good-bye to their little ones?

Feel passion and zest for life throughout your entire body. The fiery moments of a passionate experience are moments of wholeness and totality.

In referring to those who express life with an attitude of the clown, the joker or the comedian, Mark Twain wrote: "Let's be thankful for the fools. If it weren't for them the rest of us could not succeed."

Most of us know only too well that it takes a cheerful attitude and a good sense of humor to get us through some difficult circumstances. Mark Twain was correct in his observation. We can also experience life less abrasively when we have someone by our side who can look at it with a sense of humor.

If you recall in the history of kings and queens, the "jester" was a significant character in the courts. They were the therapy for royalty and had the job of making sure they were perceived as having fun making fun of themselves. The "jester" was a qualified personality with great education and wisdom.

Key #143 - Having a sense of humor allows you to view the matter at hand objectively.

An issue may have many perspectives and each of us may see it from a different viewpoint. Everyone may have a different sense of humor, also.

Another great philosopher, Thomas Hobbes said: "Laughter is nothing but sudden glory arising from some sudden conception of some eminence in oneself, by comparison with the infirmity of others or with our own formerly." Thus, he points out that a sense of humor is a playful attitude toward life's seeming mistakes. Humor is a genuine sense of joy.

Mind over Matter?

Key # 144 - A life full of humor and laughter will be a long one.

Hundreds of studies have led researchers to conclude that humor and laughter can be powerful healing agents. By the same token, they have also researched the ill effects of hostility; how it can cause death for a person who insists on holding onto destructive attitudes and circumstances.

Norman Cousins' *Anatomy Of An Illness*, his personal story of recovery from a disease that had been diagnosed as irreversible, is a classic account of the healing power of laughter. Cousins attributed his healing to what he called "life-affirming emotions."

Among these inspiring and life-giving energies he listed: faith, hope, love, a sense of purpose, a strong will to live, and a capacity for fun and laughter—humor.

Cousins found himself reversing his own illness by the constant application of laughter and his humorous attitude to the seeming ill effects of life.

Don't Take Life Too Seriously

Key # 145 - No instruction book can teach you how to develop a sense of humor or change your attitude toward life.
Being happy and expressing your joyous feelings through laughter have nothing to do with learning something special. Actually it is simply a matter of letting go of unhappiness.

Tina, aloof as always, came into my shop one day and proceeded to leaf through the new style books. She was looking for change, not only in the way she wore her hair, but also in her attitude. We proceeded to work on both the new hair style she had selected, and the New Tina she was ready to install as a replacement of the other model that had become, to quote Tina, "the monster of my life." Formerly, Tina had avoided contact with others, and in relationships she tended to be defensive.

After a couple of hours Tina left the shop with a new hairstyle, a new attitude and insight about the simple concept of humor. She was ready to try out her miracles on the new world she was about to create for herself.

When we cultivate a sense of humor, we prepare the foundation of our life for growth, just as in planting a vegetable or flower garden, we prepare the soil for our seeds. What you sow, so shall you reap. If you take life too seriously, you will become unhappy and adopt an attitude of pessimism. Is it worth it?

Ann was a gregarious person; she loved to be involved in community activities. But after her divorce, she had acquired a habit of making pessimistic remarks. Ann began to gain weight, which created a vicious cycle in her new venture as a skeptic.

"What would be your simplest advice to my imprisonment?" she asked me one day.

"I will quote Marcel Proust and perhaps you will gather the treasure," I replied. " 'The real voyage to discovery consists not in seeking new landscapes but in having new eyes.' I certainly cannot add another word to that."

Ann agreed. She set to work, transforming her pessimistic attitude, which miraculously released her from her self-imposed fat prison.

Key # 146 - Seeds of humor will make life fruitful, a growing adventure.

You will awaken a powerful giant within when you cultivate a friendly feeling toward yourself and release those self-defeating beliefs that like a dark cloud cast shadows on a sunny day. You have been born with the mental equipment to create your life however you wish it to be. Use your imagination to make a masterpiece. "Not only is it our potential to build meaningful lives; it is our obligation to ourselves." writes Dr. Maxwell Maltz, in his book, *Creative Living For Today*. "The quest for happiness is, to so many people, a grotesque traffic jam. The motor keeps running, but the car can't move." Humor dissipates this type of frustration because it is the oil in your engine.

If you are currently unhappy, it is time to sort out the unhappy beliefs that have kept you from enjoying life. As an infant you were continually and spontaneously curious, open, always searching and welcoming new experiences; you were happy. On your road to growing up you may have heard suggestions, comments and indirect gestures indicating that a child is not able to express its joy. These influences have caused confusion in your mind. It is time to evaluate them. Decide for yourself that happiness and a genuine sense of humor are your expressions to be realized. They are your self-fulfillment, your self-worth.

You will soon discover how much you really do know, and how much joy you can feel in the act of your own expression. This is the first manifestation of a loving attitude toward yourself.

Key # 147 - *The very fiber of existence lies in the strength of complementary energies that we all bring into the world.*

You are different; you are great being different! Happiness is maintained through successful living. And successful living is in every moment that you say: "I love myself just the way I am!"

Barry Neil Kaufman, author of *Happiness Is a Choice*, writes, "We are what we are and in every way, we do the best we can, the best we know how, based on our present beliefs." It is important, therefore, that you take stock of your present beliefs. When you recognize that some of them are not bringing you the happiness you wish to maintain, you will extract those beliefs that are no longer useful in creating happiness for yourself.

Happiness is having fun; it is expressing a sense of humor that reflects to others your beliefs in happiness. People rarely succeed at anything unless they have fun doing it. If you have a loving attitude about yourself, you will be sending positive signals to the world. Others will pick up those positive vibrations and feel your happiness.

Martin Seligman, Ph.D., author of *Learned Optimism*, believes that the outlook people take toward life affects their health. He further believes that we have a choice in the matter. He states: "One of the most significant findings in psychology ... is that individuals can choose the way they think."

This was also demonstrated by Norman Cousins, who attributed his successful healing to his ability to express his emotions through humor. It is imperative to keep the creative juices of good humor going; you will need that oil in your engine.

Happiness and laughter will bring forth a garden of flowers from those seeds of humor you plant along your path. Your sense of enthusiasm and joy for life will be genuine, your bouquet exquisite!

You will be surprised how easy it is to live simply, to become uncomplicated and uncluttered. You will find that you have more openness to new insights. Your capacity to adapt to new ideas will increase and you will be aware of a deeper feeling of joy. Your inner strength will reward you with a sense of contentment and you will be delighted to see that you have a greater capacity for mental and spiritual flexibility.

I found as I grew older and understood life better, humor meant much more than telling jokes. It has a lot to do with how you feel about yourself after you let go of unhappiness and all the baggage it carries.

Negative Humor Eats Away at Life

Key # 148 - Cynicism and hostility toward others create a cesspool that becomes a pit for enthusiasm and humor to stumble into.

At Duke University researchers found that people with a cynical or hostile attitude were five times more likely to die before the age of 50 than those who displayed good humor and a calmer and more trusting composure. In a survey of graduate students, Harvard University found that those students who displayed pessimistic attitudes and negative humor at the age of 25 experienced more severe illnesses at middle age. What does this tell you?

Our young people of today are surrounded by negative humor. By the time a young person finishes high school they have been on the receiving end of more than 100,000 put-downs, most of which are under the disguise of humor. It is no wonder that self-talk picks up negativity.

We are bombarded by invalidating humor that eventually creates patterns in our neural-net of electrical impulses. A simple gesture can trigger these electrical impulses that in turn will induce harmful chemical secretions. A simple word can cause a multitude of nullifying memories to tumble out of the neural-net database, causing us to re-create the discomfort of former experiences.

As we grow in awareness, we can start to root out these patterns and change them. A sense of humor is one of the best tools we have, for transforming down-spiraling patterns into healthy, constructive ones.

Key # 149 - Destructive humor, such as sarcasm and cynical remarks elicit contradictory responses from others.

Ultimately this leads to a dysfunctional relationship. Sometimes people tend to disguise truth in the form of jokes about others. This is an indication of lack of self-love and low self-esteem. To reverse this tendency, it is important to recognize the need to evaluate oneself, to determine where personal values lie.

Carl tended to deliver derogatory remarks about others. His personal insecurities were deeply embedded in layers of pain. Carl ended up in a corrections institution and debilitated his health to the point of developing severe anemia and a weakened immune system. Carl will have to understand much about humor before he can release his hostilities and comprehend the difference between destructive and uplifting humor and their effects on others as well as himself.

Carl's case is one of abandonment and exclusion by family and school friends. He tried to find attention and recognition in whatever way he could; but his attempts back-fired.

Six Steps to Cultivating Healthy Humor

Track yourself by following these simple suggestions:

1. Enjoy simplicity. Laugh often. Understand the seeming errors in life with good humor.
2. Allow others to experience your unique humor.
3. Become more aware of others and their humor. Is it uplifting, degrading or woeful?

4. Select carefully those with whom you will inter-relate.
5. Create your humor with an attitude of adventure and respect.
6. Connect with the universal loving mind consciously; and be joyful.

Tracking Questions

1. What feelings did you experience when you felt foolish doing something?
2. Are you willing to look at your own self in good humor?
3. How do you feel about others who do not express a sense of humor similar to yours?
4. How does enthusiasm help you in developing your sense of humor?
5. Can you name two great thinkers who have influenced you in cultivating your creative abilities?
6. How long has it been since you read a book of uplifting humorous adventures?

Tracking Exercises

1. Describe a situation in which your sense of humor has assisted you.
2. Describe how your sense of humor is different from that of a sibling or your parents.
3. Define the characteristics of tolerance, acceptance and respect.
4. Prepare a written outline of how you will improve your sense of humor.
5. Go as far back as you can in your memory and describe how you felt as a happy child.
6. List six ways you find your humor different from others in your working environment or social group.

Chapter 9

The Illusion of Dependency

"We are never deceived; we deceive ourselves."

— Goethe

Often we unconsciously enter into dependent, or more accurately, co-dependent relationships. Although these associations with others may appear to be strong and stable, a culprit is lurking in the shadows. This rogue subtly depletes the life force of both members of the relationship. The outcome can only be destructive to one's value or self-worth.

Note the business executive who performs required duties effectively while executing the role of being in charge. This role gives that person a sense of being in control and "on top of things."

Notice how this attitude of leadership "bleeds" into the personal relationship when a second party is willing to allow this authoritarian behavior and attitude to take over. A tyrannical personality soon becomes aggressive and overpowers the meekness of another. The natural struggle that ensues, in order to gain balance, causes this false sense of stability eventually to topple.

Respect: Fruit of Sovereignty and Saving Grace

Key # 150 - Self-respect, self-esteem and self-determination are the seeds of independence and the fruits of sovereignty that allow a person to develop autonomy.

A person of high self-esteem naturally seeks out relationships that are respectful and that provide a nurturing foundation for healthy spiritual growth.

A client named Chuck told me his interesting story about self-respect:

"I soon realized that Lana was getting stronger at playing the role of the 'weak princess,'" he said sadly. "I was noticing my own aggressiveness developing right before my eyes."

"How did you recognize this pattern?" I asked.

"Wow! It was difficult to ignore the feeling of discomfort that crept in. I felt a twinge, a sort of hint of self-deceptiveness. I wasn't sure what was occurring," confessed Chuck.

"Were you able to quickly evaluate what was happening to you?"

"Yes. I knew right away that my life had taken a turn in a direction I'd rather not follow," answered Chuck. "Soon things became very clear to me and I decided to do what it took to change the factors that were causing both Lana and me to become destructive in our own relationship."

Those steps that Chuck took and that you can take, too, if you find yourself in a co-dependent relationship, will be discussed in this chapter.

In a co-dependant relationship one tends to feel a need to have control over another. This feeling of power is a false security that is destructive to the health of any relationship.

Some signs of an imbalanced state of being that can lead to co-dependency are:

• Suppression of emotions
• Inability to verbally express one's feelings

- Obsessive urge for development
- Constant striving for perfection
- Excessive strong self-discipline
- Fanatical adherence to a given theory
- Self-reproach with the perception of having fallen short of ideals
- Prejudice
- Cowardice
- Insistence on being right
- Acceptance of ignorance without seeking for answers

Independence Is Not Isolation

Do independent people isolate themselves in some way, to avoid the possibilities of co-dependency? Does a person who is independent have to pull away from the natural flow of life? Is independence difficult to attain?

Key # 151 - Independence is the state of resting well-assured upon the centeredness of one's inner light.

Independence is simply a state of being "in-ner" dependent or dependent on the inner spark and not getting entangled in the dramas of others. Independence has nothing to do with a "leave me alone" attitude. On the contrary: An independent person has the strength to "leave alone" the issues of others.

Independent individuals do not pull away from intimate relationships; instead they complement and add energy to them. I have a couple of friends I will call Vincent and Rosie who are a model of independence in their relationship with each other. In spite of their outgoing nature, they seem to have acquired their independence in other relationships as well. Vincent owns his own business and Rosie is a service provider in a retirement center.

Vincent is well liked by his employees and has a knack for getting others to be happy about performing their tasks well as

a team. Sales have increased steadily, making Vincent financially stable. He does not allow the reactions of others to get
him entangled in subtle disagreements. He does not discuss
business challenges with Rosie.

Likewise, she keeps her home life positive and healthy.
Both have a deep respect for each other's personal space and
sense of freedom. Rosie and Vincent have found the secret to
independence: self-love.

The Sting of Co-Dependency

Co-dependency has a wretched sting. The travesty lies in the
apparent feeling of strength that seems to flourish at the onset
of a relationship but that eventually becomes a lodestone that
will carry one to the depths of a deep unforgiving ocean of
despair.

Symptoms of co-dependency are deceptive and irregular.
Dependent individuals feel strong as a result of being a part
of one another. They feel supported and loved. Yet when
required to survive on their own, their weakness surfaces.
Denial, blame of the other and destructive behaviors feed the
co-dependency.

Dependency often leads to the use of coping mechanisms
or substitutes that cover up insecurities and lack of self-esteem.
These mechanisms can be food, alcohol, prescriptive or recre-
ational drugs, or other addictive behavior such as shopping,
talking on the phone, sex, etc. Co-dependency cycles must be
broken if already in place, and avoided if not contaminated
already.

My client Margo is forever talking about her perfect man. She
is a bright college girl who is conscious of her appearance. She
makes her hair appointments well ahead of time to make certain that her hair always looks well groomed. One afternoon,
while I was styling her hair, she told me an unusual story.

"You won't believe what a devastating experience I just had last week!" she exclaimed.

"Well, by the sound of your voice and the downcast expression on your face it *must* have been devastating. What have the ides of March brought to you?" I tried to humor her a bit, since I realized how upset she was.

"I have to admit, it was just like you had said. The wages of an addictive co-dependent relationship are very unfulfilling," said Margo. "Pierre was a gentleman in every way, but there were 'ulterior motives' behind his attention. I was unaware of his hidden agendas, so I became 'hooked' on his caring for me."

"But you can't always tell when it's a 'game,'" I responded.

"I know that now. But while I was the 'princess' and he was such a 'knight' I wasn't careful enough to notice his dishonesty." Margo wiped a tear with the tissue I handed her.

"Margo," I reassured her, "you are so much stronger for having had this experience! It has restored your self-respect. You've come away a little bruised, yes. But you now have the fortitude to resume a much happier life. Think of the wisdom you've gained!"

We gave each other a hug. "A Beautiful You has emerged!" I declared. "What do you think of the new style I've created for you today?" I handed her the mirror.

"Thank you, I love it!" Her spirits noticeably brightened. "I've treated myself nicely in more ways than one."

Just like Margo, we can show independence and self-respect by taking the steps necessary to walk away from a relationship that is not conducive to a healthy friendship. All of us can emerge from co-dependent relationships with more wisdom.

Co-dependent abusive relationships with hidden agendas tend to make a person feel in control of what is going on, making it difficult to notice anything amiss. The abuser is falsely fulfilled, convinced that the other has "bought the goods." That fixation causes a rush. When attempt to gain control begins to break down, the seeming "victim" suddenly feels a loss of caring by the other. Thus begins a vicious cycle of compensating for this inadequacy. The game of "power struggle" follows. Feelings of insecurity now awakened, cause one or the other to hold on to what once was sensed as a strong bonding. This becomes the illusion of the past and the relationship suffers from what I call "partnership hemorrhaging."

Isla, a small frail girl, comes in to get a permanent about three times a year. I enjoy her company while she is in the salon. She is a caring and loving person.

"I have a sister who can't seem to find herself a nice guy to stay with," she said one day, as soon as she found a comfortable chair to sit on. She was eager to share her most compelling thoughts this morning.

"You are concerned about your sister in Colorado?"

"Yes. I've been thinking a lot about her after our last telephone conversation. It appears to me that she tends to weaken her self-respect when a good-looking guy comes on to her. She likes to hold on to those guys who give her special attention. She's so focused on their good looks, other more valuable character traits don't matter to her so much. This is going to be her demise, I just know it!" she exclaimed.

"Sounds like you are very much involved emotionally in her affairs," I commented.

"I tend to do that with her, I'm worried for her." Isla softened her voice and continued, "What can I do for her?"

I thought quickly and simply replied, "Allow her to go through her experiences. She is creating her world, and the wisdom she will extract from the experiences she brings into her reality will be her reward. Your treasure lies in the love you have for her through the respect you extend to her."

"I do love and respect her," sighed Isla.

Isla may have heard and understood my words. Possibly that gave her relief from her concerns. But the test will come when she has to live the wisdom of those words. Why is it so difficult sometimes to let go?

Are You Tempted to Take Care of the Problems of Others?

Key # 152 - Difficulty in letting go of concern for others is founded in a need or desire to control others.

Holding on to such dispositions causes the destructive cycle of subtle co-dependency. It is this attachment, wanting to take care of others and wanting to solve their problems for them, that causes the care-giver to become weak, stale, de-energized and depleted of self-worth. Neither party really evolves from this attitude. To dissolve co-dependent addictions before moving on, a forgiving heart must come into play.

Key # 153 - Love people as they are, without trying to fix them.

This is called unconditional love. Complex situations arise when we are unable to define what the attachment factor might be. We tend to depend on past experiences to resolve the situation at hand. Insisting on old patterns will only cause more relationship dependency.

If you call yourself a "care-taker," a "worrier," a "sucker," or a "softie," you are in a co-dependent relationship with a fixation on "being the nice guy."

One of the factors involved in wanting so desperately to see others grow or not get hurt, is a need to have people act in a particular way. It can also be the yearning desire to have them appreciate us or our belief systems. Detaching ourselves emotionally from others does not mean we do not love them. It means we are allowing them to become responsible for their own lives. We are setting them free. Our benefit will

be felt in the release of a dull pressure and the feeling of freedom we subtly experience. The energy we gain is reward
enough.

We cannot overlook the reactions we will sense from others.
They may insist that we are not caring enough about them. We
only have to go within for affirmation and strength. We only
have to follow our loving heart.

Is the Opinion of Others Really That Important?

How do we truly feel about the opinions of others? How are we
able to process their comments and their re-actions to our
changes? If you find yourself toying with the illusion of fulfillment when others cheer you on or pat you on the back
for doing something, ask yourself why you are relishing these
gestures. Are you in need of this response from others, or are
you judging yourself about something? You may have a need to
be reassured by others. If you are judging yourself and looking
for some form of justification, you are in a co-dependent pattern.

Perhaps you are reflecting on "right" or "wrong" choices.
If so, you are judging yourself and have found yourself being
swallowed by polarities. Polarities have their place for building
character. But to become engulfed in the destructive cycle of
comparisons is to become co-dependent and thus, lacking in
self-worth.

These behaviors cause heaviness of heart and depleted
energy. They consume your self-value and invite feelings of
failure. A feather-like heart is far lighter than praise and honor
from others. Trust your inner guidance for reassurance and
you will no longer find yourself entering into co-dependant
relationships.

Participation in Relationships Is Life!

The thrill of being alive comes from involving ourselves actively in life with others. We can't just sit and watch the game. We must get out there in the field and play! Involvement in relationships that sap our life-giving energies is not the ticket to joy or a fulfilling life.

Key # 154 - To become actively involved with what is happening around us includes being receptive.

It also involves being aware of the health of that involvement with others. Again, we are talking about self-knowledge, self-control and self-respect.

Unfortunately, for some people, listening to their conscience is like "taking advice from a total stranger." Be assured that if you take your daily strolls through the caves of inner solitude, you will know yourself and harbor no doubts about your life's purpose.

My friend Dee always was ready to party at the drop of a hat. She loved getting involved with people and participating in community activities. One of her phone conversations to me was memorable.

"Why is it that I always get volunteered for the job?" Dee complained.

"Is it that you give others the impression that you like to get involved, so they give you the job?" I offered.

"Well, I'm discovering that I'm not appreciated even if I do a great job."

"Dee, I'd like to say that if you notice your self value deteriorating from all of this, it's normal."

"Really?" She paused, waiting for me to give her some bits of wisdom.

"I'm sure you already know this. You just haven't taken the time to give yourself a moment of self-appreciation."

"What should I do now?"

"Take a deep look within and find the spark that has been buried under the rubble of taking care of others. That's where you'll find your answers. Value yourself just as you are, and you will discover why it is that everyone loves to have you around."

"I feel better already!" exclaimed Dee. "How can others appreciate me when I can't even appreciate myself? I'm definitely going to make some changes. Thank you!"

I could tell from the tone of Dee's voice that the heaviness had lifted. One day in the mail a thank you note arrived with a drawing of a smiley face.

Am I My Best Friend?

Often the relationship that goes undetected and undernourished is the one we have with ourselves. The treatment we give ourselves speaks of how we value ourselves in relationship with others. Subtle habits such as statements made in a joking fashion, or revealed through a nervous gesture, tend to deliver the way we treat ourselves.

Key # 155 - When we become more aware of the relationship we have with ourselves we will discover the source of our self-worth.

Terry, Laura and I were at the golf shooting range one sunny afternoon. After a few holes we paused for a break.

"Tricked you, didn't I?" declared Terry to Laura, a triumphant gleam in her eye.

"You certainly did; but I can take it!" was Laura's meek response.

"You mean you didn't tell Laura you were bringing her to the range?" I asked Terry.

"I guess I'm a 'bad girl' now," retorted Terry, ignoring my inquiry.

"No," I responded, "it's not about being 'good' or 'bad;' it's about respecting her trust in you." I continued.

"Oh! So you're now judging me?" Terry accused.

"Stop, you guys!" Laura pleaded, attempting to dismiss the situation. "I really don't care!"

"Laura," I held her by the shoulders, "the way you respond to the way others treat you has a lot to do with how you value yourself. So, think about it before you go and say that it doesn't matter."

I jumped off the grass and picked up a driver club to continue our golf practice.

Laura turned to Terry. "Terry, it does matter to me how you feel and how you treat me. Please let's not let this come between our friendship. Maybe we can talk about this later. Let's finish our game for now."

"Laura, I'm sorry. Yes, I would like to discuss this later. I didn't know I was so insensitive. Thank you. I needed that attitude adjustment." Grinning sheepishly, Terry placed a golf ball on the tee pin.

Key #156 - Weak relationships with others stem from a weak relationship with ourselves.

A strong foundation of self-worth allows us to move with ease toward the fulfillment we desire, happily accomplishing the life purpose we have chosen. In a focused direction, momentum will naturally pick up. When you consider your progress and view yourself as worthy, you acquire a power that will propel you into relationships worthy of positive, joyful results. Allow the magic to take over.

Stay Focused on Your Dream!

Stay focused on your dream and your life purpose. Diverting your attention only pulls away from the strong focus of bringing a desired outcome into your reality. A healthy relationship with yourself and others is a life-giving energy that moves you through the world of happiness and fulfillment. Once the outcome you desire is a part of your physical reality, your attention may be directed toward a new dream. But first you must stay focused on Dream Number One, to avoid splitting your energy.

Key # 157 - Creating independent relationships requires a sharpened vision that is devoid of co-dependent irregularities.

Remember the story of the bundle of sticks that was strong together but weakened as they were separated?

Only after you have attained the initial focus of self-worth does independence come, as you refresh your mind with new ideas. Focusing on your vision first keeps you from splitting your valuable creative energy. The sustaining of a dream and active participation in it are uncovered treasures of your destiny. The growth intermittently taking place is a natural development.

Key # 158 - Independence doesn't just happen; it happens just.

Maintaining an inner peace crowns the outcome as it blossoms.

Family Responses Can Make or Break You

Key #159 - Self-esteem and independence are closely tied to family and environment.

The initial influences in your life (how others have listened to you, whether or not they have taken you seriously, whether or not you were genuinely cared for, etc.) made an important impression on attaining your dreams and establishing your relationships.

If your family experiences of the past have provided you with high self-worth and personal dignity, you are more capable of making decisions concerning appropriate relationships.

Not too long ago my daughter, Cami, who is 32, eagerly shared with me one of her most enlightening experiences.

"I'm so glad we had parents who fortified our self-worth. Thank you, Mom." She gave me a hug and kissed my cheek affectionately.

"You're very welcome, of course!" I laughed, giving her a hug and kiss in return.

"Fighting within the judicial system and going through this long divorce process with a child custody battle is not fun," she admitted.

"You have really been spending unending amounts of effort in this." I gave her hand a squeeze. Cami had always been one of the most sensitive and vulnerable of my children.

"I discovered the nature of my own relationship in the most unusual way," she continued. "The fight was devouring much of my time and money. It seemed to be unending. Then one day I stopped and let myself think about what I was doing. My fighting hadn't resolved these civil matters; they just kept extending things. It wasn't until considered my own self-worth and humbled myself to accept the consequences of what I had created, that I started to appreciate the value in respecting myself. I gave up the judicial battle. Once I started to cherish and value myself, I discovered I'd had enough of the courts. No one, including the courts, was going to take my dignity away from me!" Cami declared.

"And then came the relief and a quicker solution to the years of struggle," I smiled.

"I think I found out who I was and how much joy there could be, in loving myself."

I was proud of my daughter. "You won the fight; there are no more personal sacrifices." "Do you know what else I learned?" exclaimed Cami. "I will never put someone else in any position that I wouldn't want to experience."

"That sounds like the Golden Rule," I responded. "I can feel your love for self and also for your children and your ex-husband," Tears of gratitude misted the eyes of both mother and daughter.

Comparison Is a Vicious Cycle

Key #160 - Comparing yourself to others, your former self or your "ideal" self for the purpose of pronouncing "judgments" is a vicious cycle of sabotage.

It serves no purpose except to tear you down to yourself. This attitude makes you vulnerable to co-dependencies. Instead, feel the freedom and the strength in having been through an experience that has served you well. Be the best you know how to be. Strive for excellence within yourself and release the need to compare yourself to anyone.

When in doubt about the nature of your relationships, test yourself by using the lessons learned from past experiences. This is your wisdom library. Remember: wisdom is crystal clear and void of any emotional element. You will not feel emotionally stimulated by memories of the past when you view them objectively.

Use the past as a key to unlock a brighter future. Extract the "moral of the story," and move on with determination and self-esteem.

One of my clients, Avalon, did just that. I was very busy the day Avalon dropped in for a hair cut, but he decided to wait his turn. I was happy he did. He had an interesting story to share with me that illustrates how someone can detect co-dependent relationships. Avalon consciously adjusted his own attitudes and noticed the results.

Avalon sat in the styling chair and gave his instructions on how he wanted his hair cut, "The same as last time. You did such a nice job. Use the number two guard on the sides and back, and then the rest short with the scissors."

I proceeded as directed and inquired, "So how are things with you, Avalon?"

Immediately he exclaimed, "I finally got tired of not being appreciated, so I changed some things."

I wondered just what sort of things he could be talking about, remembering the last conversation we'd had a couple of weeks ago. "So what exactly did you do?" I asked.

"Ginny has always expected me to bail her out of her financial situations that I felt were unnecessarily created. She has a tendency to give money to someone else in need. I was wondering what to do about this because it was not the type of relationship I wanted to establish with a girl I would marry."

"So what did you discover from changing your behavior?" I queried.

"I found that Ginny and I were in a co-dependent relationship because I wanted her to like me for being the nice guy, and she wanted me to like her because she was the nice girl who always was helping others."

"How do you two get along now?" I set to work, following his instructions.

"Well, actually we don't. Ginny decided to break up. She didn't like the 'new me.' Or, I should say, the 'real me.' But I was happy to find myself strong in what was important to me. I like being independent and I guess she doesn't. It's that simple."

Avalon did seem different this time—lighter; as if a burden had been lifted from him. I could tell he had made a decision that was right for him.

"Wow! You really have made a change," I exclaimed. "I'm glad to see that young people can be proud of themselves and value their self-worth." I brushed his neck, removed the cape from his shoulders and handed him the mirror.

"Well, I have you to thank. Yes, I do," he declared, plucking his cowboy hat off the rack.

Ginny's behavior of helping others was not to help them help themselves but only to make herself look good in the eyes of the man she wanted to marry. Actually she turned out doing just the opposite, since she was destroying her own financial resources by giving away money she needed herself.

Ginny had also creating another potential problem. Eventually when she cut off her charity toward others, since her relationship with them depended on her gifts, they would probably discard her.

Key # 161 - Helping others help themselves is a form of self-love and self-worth.
When we help others to recognize abundance and happiness, we bring wealth and joy into our own life. We must be careful not to feel we need to give them abundance and happiness; we are not responsible for their resourcefulness. This is their department.

Can You Receive Comfortably?

Key #162 - When relationships have a good "giver" and an uncomfortable "receiver," they become unhealthy and co-dependent.
Note the way relationships become distorted when the "giver" continues to give and the "receiver" is unwilling to comfortably receive. The receiver becomes a "taker" and makes remarks such as: "You don't need to do that!" Or: "You shouldn't have!" Or: "You didn't need to spend the money on me!"

The "giver" soon becomes exhausted. Even compliments may be received with such statements as: "Ah, it's just an old thing. I've had it for years." Or: "It's really nothing great."

If the "receiver" and the "giver" are both reciprocating, they form a healthy bonding relationship. Each is a sincere "giver" and "receiver" with willingness to establish independence, love and firm self-worth.

We must first ask ourselves: Have we been true to ourselves and honest with our evaluation of how we see those with whom we are in relationship? Then proceed with the next question: Have we been giving of ourselves without hidden agendas?

Dishonesty and ulterior motives destroy the efforts of giving help to others. Once we have determined our self-worth and how we give and receive, we will go forth with a plan.

Want Changes? It Takes 21 Days to Form a Habit

Key # 163 - A valuable way to stay on track with a plan is to monitor your conscious efforts for 21 days.

The period of 21 days is crucial. It has been established by professionals of human behavior that it takes 21 days to acquire a new habit—to set it in place as an attitude.

Remember the way our mind works? Do you recall the way those neural-net connections, the pathways that are most easily trodden by memory, continue to follow the same route? When we retrace our steps for 21 days with the serious intent of forming a habit, we fortify our neural connections. They respond favorably when we need them to deliver positive support for our newly created experiences.

By using your journal, keep track of the new habits you wish to acquire. Note your progress in 21 days. Make sure you keep records of your feelings during this period. This will give you a better picture of how you have come to form a habit you have desired with a passion.

Hidden Issues

Key #164 - When we go within and allow ourselves to consider our vulnerabilities we become empowered by a sense of dignity.

In this state of powerful self-respect, lack of confidence dissolves. We regain the strength that once was ours. You are using the same behavior as when you come up to a railroad tracks: Stop! Look! and Listen! Stop to notice where you are. Look at the possibilities that lie ahead; they could be disastrous if you remain in a co-dependent relationship, or favorable for recovery if you decide to free yourself. Listen to your inner guidance for directions on how to proceed on your personally designed journey.

Know that co-dependency is not irreversible; it is not even a sin. Becoming aware of its destructive nature can be a fun thing to do if you take the attitude of playing the game of starving the "dependency worm" who loves to live in damp and dark places.

Key # 165 - Breaking co-dependency can easily be called the invisible new road.

Remember, images are the keys to the invisible world. The first step on that road is to create the "images" you prefer. The second step is to bring them to the forefront of your mind. This will assist in forming a different reality.

Starving the "worm" begins by cutting off its supply of feelings of superiority, sweet talking, being the "good do-bee," covering up for the other guy, punishing yourself for taking the blame, and other destructive alternatives to self-respect. All of these attitudes feed the "co-dependency worm." Shine the warm loving light of your inner wisdom on this insidious worm and watch it shrivel and dry up, and die.

Gender Issues

Key # 166 - Gender issues usually lie hidden in a co-dependent relationship.

These issues are related to the gender labeling of actions taken by the other person. Regardless of who is the accuser, the habit of assigning certain attitudes to males or females is just that: a habit. These dispositions are personality traits usually acquired by the person either by observation or dependence on role models.

I often hear comments such as: "She's just a dumb woman"; or: "It's just like a man!" Comments such as these are spoken by those with hidden insecurities.

To overcome these gender issues, communicate with your partner. For instance, if you find yourself commenting that a person does things in a certain way because they are male or female, confront this attitude with the other person and discuss the underlying factors involved.

Lucy had always believed that her husband responded in a defensive way to her comments because he was a stubborn man. "Just like a man!" she'd say. "Always thinking they have to be right."

Lucy decided she was tired of his defensive attitude because it really never gave her the opportunity to truly express herself or deliver her full point of view.

Can you see what is brewing here? Her husband's habit of defensiveness was feeding his purpose. He didn't have to hear her out. It wasn't because he was a tough man. A woman can use the same attitude and will be called "an obstinate woman." You see, it really isn't about gender.

Here's another story to illustrate my point.

Leonard commented, "She's just like a woman, can't follow directions." Leonard got the results he put forth in his co-dependent relationship. Lucy couldn't follow any of his directions. Leonard was domineering and Carolyn was playing the "poor me" victim role. She chose Leonard for a partner because she loved to be dominated by "leader/police" men.

Carolyn was also unaware of her own insecurities and issues with gender: Woman were conceptualized as weak, meek and dependent. Men were determined, bold and protective. This formed the perfect environment for the co-dependent relationship to germinate.

Before engaging in a healthy relationship, both personalities must establish strong feelings of self-worth. One does not need to lord over a weak, frail, incapable "female." The female does not need to be protected by a "male" bully or demanding bull. You can revise the genders to find hen-pecked men and women who are humorously pictured wielding rolling pins over the heads of their mates.

You Must Passionately Desire a Healthy Relationship

Key # 167 - A healthy independent relationship develops when a person has a passion for creating one.

It's that simple.

Co-dependency is not a sin. It is merely something that can happen to us because we have been blind to our defensive habits. We may have created patterns of behavior that at one time seemed like the only way out of a painful circumstance.

As we become more aware and mature we incorporate the wisdom extracted from our past experiences. We become capable of evaluating our life's experiences from moment to moment. We delete unhealthy habits, retaining characteristics that feed our lives with bliss and self value. We respect everyone—including ourselves; and we continue to be grateful for the experiences we bring into our lives as part of the adventure we have chosen.

Self-Referral vs. Object Referral

Key # 168 - Happiness is a "self-referral" effort.

If we are to depend on someone or something else to determine how we feel about our life, the outcome of this "object referral" will predictably cause discomfort that can ultimately lead to disaster. Here's a story to illustrate this point:

> A handsome young boy was sad because he didn't have a pony. His parents got him a pony; he became elated and rode to his heart's content. Going too fast around a corner caused him to fall off the pony and break his leg. The boy and his parents were now very sad because his leg was broken. His leg healed and the young boy once more was happy. He grew up and went to sea; this made him sad to leave his home. He found a beautiful girl in a faraway land

and was very happy. He married the girl and experienced a new feeling of joy. She fell ill and died. He was now very sad. But she left him a healthy young son who once again filled his father's life with joy. The handsome man was so worn from the stress of his life that he never lived long enough to see his own son marry.

You see how the cycle of happiness and sadness continued for someone who referred to outside sources to determine his joy. Had this young boy known that his Nirvana was always within himself, regardless of his environmental circumstances, he could have conserved his peace of mind and possibly lived longer.

What is the "moral" of the story? The emotional roller-coaster of stress and disappointment is unnecessary. A deep emotional experience is essential for extracting wisdom from life, but not by extracting life from our emotional experiences.

Below is a list of other patterns of behavior that often hold people back:

- Indecisiveness
- Arguing with others
- Feeling worse after you become angry
- Getting along poorly with others
- Irritability
- Stubbornness
- Rash behavior
- Contrary-ness
- Emotional outbursts
- Mood swings
- Suppressing emotions
- Angering easily
- Easily agitated and distressed
- Jealousy

Companion or Competitor?

Co-dependent relationships often come in candy-coated forms. In the rush of getting our own insecurity issues settled into a nest or peaceful retreat, we can become competitors in a relationship instead of companions. Co-dependent relationships many times begin when we allow another person to feel stronger and thus have an illusion of independence. The competition games initially may be subtle; they do have their motives.

If you see a destructive pattern forming, you will know it is the sign of an insecurity. The net result will be a co-dependency.

Determine now if you are a competitor or a companion in a relationship. Perhaps at times you are both. Do you want control? If so, ask yourself, "Why do I feel the necessity to have control? Do I feel inferior?"

While I was finishing up Pat's hair-do one Saturday morning, Fred, her husband, burst out, "I was the sort of guy who needed to make sure everything was under control. Little did I know that this was putting more stress in my life than necessary, until I had a heart attack and hit bottom. I sure did some thinking during those days in the hospital.

"I discovered that it was not worth my life to feel I had to be in such a controlling position. I had actually never appreciated my wife's strength, and how she could really manage very well without me. I sure took notice and destroyed that stress that was eating away at my relationship. Not to mention what it was doing to my health."

"Were you feeling competition from your wife at some point?" I inquired, curious to know what had brought about this enlightenment.

"He just liked to feel and act macho," declared Pat.

"She's right," confessed Fred. "I thought that was important. The truth is, I felt insecure about some things. I made myself become a competitor to my own insecurity."

"I'm glad he changed to being my loving companion. He's really a nice guy," said Pat. "It's just too bad that it took a heart attack for him to clarify his mind!"

Nothing more needed to be said. Their confession delivered the picture of two people who had released their co-dependency and were grateful for their fresh start.

Key # 169 - In order to develop a secure relationship with yourself it is necessary to become responsible for your own experiences.

It is also necessary to discover how you have brought these experiences to yourself.

Taking responsibility for having created your life has an uncanny way of producing self-evaluation. Self-responsibility allows you to remove yourself from the scene and become an observer of the experience without the burden of emotional luggage. Try it; you'll like it!

Key # 170 - Begin your relationships by communicating your feelings in words that say exactly how you feel.

Become more sensitive to your own vocabulary by selecting words that authentically express your feelings. Ask questions to learn if the other person understands you. Take time to explore new ways of expressing yourself. These factors will lead to healthy relationships.

Key # 171 - Avoid behaviors that bring personal gain.

These behaviors indicate that you have issues of unworthiness and the need to control others. Hidden agendas and ulterior motives are like termites, destroying the foundation of what you have already built. They also quash the trust that holds relationships together. Becoming aware of these factors in your own behavior will deliver the hidden motives of the other person.

You must level honestly with yourself before you begin to communicate with others. Allow others to express themselves until you can understand each other.

Detach yourself from other people's situations. Remember, they are creating for themselves what they have chosen to experience. Your responsibility lies in staying clear of any "guilt trip" that indicates a co-dependent relationship.

And last but not least, stop defending your point of view!

How to Break the Cycle of Co-Dependency

How can we tell the difference between co-dependent and independent relationships?

One day I was invited to participate in a group therapy session with men and women who had come together for help in releasing co-dependent relationships.

"The one principle we all need to remember," I began, "is that the 'reference point' to all relationships begins at home, within us. We must hold ourselves responsible for our relationships, regardless of how we may come to judge them or come to feel about them."

"What do you mean?" inquired one of the participants.

"It is necessary to have a 'point of reference' any time you are building something. Note the way a developer begins his work. He first must set a reference point and make alignments and measurements from there. So it is with our life. We must begin to consciously have a 'point of reference' to guide all other points." I illustrated on the chalk board by drawing a stick with a string drawn from it to another stick.

"How do you do that?" asked one of the members.

"When you can become conscious enough of the power that is within you," I continued, "you will know that no one else can make you do or be anything you do not allow. This means that once this 'point of reference' has been established—your inner spark, you will feel a sense of security and empowerment within and without. You will never feel abandonment or insecurity."

"Is it like being independent within yourself?" asked a young girl who was sitting in the front row.

"Yes. That's good!" I praised her and continued, "Possibly if you are acquainted with the Scriptures, you know that phrase about listening to the still small voice within. Right?" I fixed my gaze on an older fellow sitting by the window.

"Yeah, yeah," he agreed after a moment.

"Okay, now that we realize that our 'point of reference' is ourselves, we can go from there and say the strength of that point lies in understanding that we are sovereign individuals. This sovereignty means that we are the supreme independent and unlimited authority for directing our lives. We make the ultimate decision about what happens to us in relationships and how we go about choosing them."

"What about Our Heavenly Father being the ultimate authority?" inquired the young girl again.

"If you were the parent, would you not allow your child to learn by personal experiences?" I made the analogy.

"I would," she said firmly.

"Okay; being a sovereign individual begins with taking responsibility for your own relationships," I reiterated, opening the dictionary to my marked page.

"What about the way others make us feel like 'victims' of their manipulations?" asked one of the others.

"You must remember your 'point of reference' and ask yourself if it is at all possible to become a 'victim of circumstances' when you are exercising your sovereignty. You have to be conscious and aware of your own power and not allow someone else to overcome you. That's why it's important to track your self-worth!" I responded.

I asked one of the participants to read the definition of sovereign:

"Sovereign. Person supreme in power." She stopped and looked around at the others as she handed back the dictionary.

"So," I continued, "the bottom line is: We can be in control of our own lives by being sovereign and not creating co-dependent relationships any more. It isn't that we stumble into them. We have simply forgotten to be consciously responsible for the outcome of our lives."

"How can we keep from falling into co-dependent relationships?" asked another.

"Thank you for asking. This brings me to the six suggestions I have developed as a guide."

I proceeded to the chalk board on the wall. "Here they are, for you to copy down if you wish. The belief you have about your abilities and your potential is the key, so align yourself with these six suggestions." I wrote the following on the board:

Six Guidelines for Healthy Relationships

1. **Commitment** – Commit to be kind to yourself and others under all circumstances.
2. **Appreciation** – Think and talk constructively about yourself and others at all times.
3. **Communication** – Learn to listen well. Take time to evaluate your thoughts and actions. Be honest and express with the other person(s) those thoughts that relate to them.
4. **Quality Time** – Give yourself quality time to focus on your dream. Quantity of time is also important. These moments do not just happen; they must be planned. You will then be ready to give quality time to others.
5. **Coping Ability** – What appears to be "difficult" may be the very thing required to get you over an issue you have not resolved. When these difficult times happen, stay calm. They occur to make you stronger and bring you the wisdom you seek. They can destroy a weak person. When you love yourself, you will not consciously create anything that will hurt you. Maintain your balance by going within.

6. **Spiritual Wellness or Well-Being** – Remain centered within your own power and commit to virtues such as: integrity, honesty, loyalty and conscientiousness.

I concluded the session by inviting the participants to project their new dream publicly, as a means of vocalizing their commitments to remain independent. I encouraged them to stay in tune with their "point of reference" in order to become more aware of how to detect co-dependency.

I suggested that a great way to refresh the mind about sovereignty is to read about the lives of those who have made a mark in history. "Their stories of inner strength will serve as an inspiration," I told them.

"Remember," I concluded, "it takes 21 days to establish a firm pattern of changes, so give yourselves time to incorporate these new ideas into your regimen."

Before I closed the session I thanked all of them for being so special.

Tracking Questions

1. How do you feel about your conditioned responses to letting go?
2. What two things would you like to let go of today?
3. Do you find yourself feeling responsible for making other peoples' lives work?
4. Do you feel uncomfortable about assessing your relationships? Why? Why not?
5. How do you feel about yourself after finding yourself in a co-dependent relationship?
6. Have you noticed any co-dependent issues in your self? List some.

Tracking Exercises

1. Write a one-page description of your sovereignty as an individual.

2. Evaluate your present relationship(s) and write down the issues you see the other person(s) have. Note these issues as your own, because we are all experiencing difficulties with the very thing others are bringing into focus for us.
3. How would you describe the "pebble in your shoe"?
4. List five statements you use that describe gender issues.
5. Make a list of ten qualities you will adopt in order to become more of a companion and less of a competitor in your relationship(s).
6. Write a paragraph about how you will break yourself from participating in any type of co-dependent relationship. Make an outline of your plan.

Chapter 10

Self-Fulfillment Is a Process, Not a Destination

"To travel hopefully is a better thing
than to arrive."

— Robert Louis Stevenson

What does it mean to become self-fulfilled?

I was a typical "over-achiever" who at a certain point in my life believed I had finally accomplished my goals. The problem was: I still had not found inner peace and self-satisfaction. In fact, like others who declare to themselves that they've finally "made it," I became intoxicated with this false feeling of success to the point where it started to become self-destructive. At a certain point, I found it physically impossible to keep up with myself!

My customers had a pet name for me: "super woman." I was trying to do it all: run three businesses, raise seven children, run a home school program, assist my children with their professional music careers, volunteer my time in community programs, tutor Spanish classes ... the list goes on. I found myself depleted and felt "used."

My self-worth tracking program will prevent you from falling into this nasty habit of thinking you have to "do it all" in order to feel self-fulfilled and accomplished.

Key # 172 - The nature of evolution is to progress ourselves toward the ability to self-reflect.

Walking in the light does not negate the existence of darkness. Rather it brings vision into the darkness we often walk through. The light within illuminates the way, allowing us to see where we are going. And if happiness is what we are ready to experience, we must turn on the light!

Too often we hear about success, fulfillment, relationships and careers being a destination. In truth, the journey of life is about enjoying the moment; it is about self-fulfillment in the NOW.

The fact that most people fail to see themselves in joy is self-evident if you check the statistics of our country's health. Most of this is basically due to the outlook toward life as a destination (one to be worried about), as unknown as that might be, and not as a journey to be lived joyfully from day to day on the path of eternity.

Key # 173 - Success is the product of success.

The more one succeeds, the better one feels. The better one feels, the more success one is capable of attaining. We tend to do better after we have witnessed successful outcomes. Strength is gained in taking the first steps necessary to accomplishing something we most desire.

Henry David Thoreau says it well: "If one advances confidently in the direction of his dreams, and endeavors to live the life which he has imagined, he will meet with a success unexpected in common hours. He will pass an invisible boundary; new, universal, and more liberal laws will begin to establish themselves around and within him; and he will live with the license of a higher order of beings."

I believe life is a process of spiritual evolution; and since everything is spiritual before it becomes physical (energy before it becomes matter) spirituality encompasses all aspects of existence.

Key # 174 - Love is the propelling force behind the desire to evolve.

Love is behind the passion to grow toward something beyond where we are at the moment: wanting to be in the mountains when you are at the ocean shore, wanting to be asleep when you are awake, or healthy when you are ill. The desire to be elsewhere is natural. It is the thrust of growth and evolution.

Dr. Clinton J. Davidson of the Bell Telephone Laboratories in New York received a Nobel Prize in Physics for discovering the dual nature of the electron, with characteristics of both wave and particle. The electron has been discovered to have a Jekyll and Hyde personality!

In life's experience, we recognize that fulfillment takes on moments of journey and moments of destination simultaneously. Neither cancels out the other but, more correctly, is assimilated as making known the unknown—in bringing to light that which still remains in darkness.

Key # 175 - Our attitude often determines the outcome of a situation.

Notice any difference in "half full" or "half empty" statements? Note the emotional (feelings) reactions toward these statements. "Half full" gives the sense of approaching fulfillment, or a journey to completion, and "half empty" tends to describe an ebbing or waning of the tide. The "half empty" glass of water elicits feelings of lack—a dissatisfied customer. A certain joyful expectation accompanies the "half full" statement.

Key # 176 - Bringing up the past needn't be burdensome.

Detaching yourself emotionally from your past has a way of delivering intent and purpose. By cleaning house, you discard what you don't want or need and focus on what's necessary or basic.

Remove yourself from the emotional "baggage" of attachment in any relationship. Make relationships adventuresome.

Begin and end the adventure with honor and respect. When we treat relationships with kindness, we soon stop anticipating the end; we stop expecting a separation from such relationships.

It's sad to note that often our adventures in life "end" at some point. Notice the way humans display an expected termination of the adventure of life at some point in time. We are actually making our destiny reach an end or finishing point.

If our attitudes determine the outcome of our relationships, why should it be such a difficult task to forecast a successful outcome? Managing relationships to create outcomes that will not have complete closure but maintain some form of friendship denotes a journey in progress: the journey of loving-kindness toward another human being.

Key # 177 - *Self-fulfillment is attained by the acquisition of certain attributes that build our character.*

1. We must give ourselves a fine reputation to live up to.
2. By using self-encouragement we make faults seem easy to correct.
3. We can talk about our own mistakes and still feel good about ourselves.
4. We begin each day with honest appreciation of ourselves by praising ourselves.
5. We ask questions of ourselves that stimulate growth. We are not critical or self-judgmental.
6. We allow ourselves the benefit of the doubt by forgiving ourselves.

The following personal qualities that enhance life and relationships:

- Responsibility
- Fairness
- Respect
- Gratitude
- Peace

- Honesty
- Maturity
- Tenacity
- Integrity

If you are unfamiliar with these words, look them up. Begin to feel their value and apply their meaning to your life. These qualities develop personal strength and help to develop attitudes that will move us past the self-sabotage syndrome we often create in our journey of self-discovery.

Friendship Flourishes with Freedom to Flow

Key # 178 - Become friends first, and remain friends forever.

Extend your horizons and see yourself living forever. Then feel the difference in your attitude toward life. My special partner and I were friends first; we developed a rich friendship without the heated lusting after one another. This initiated a lasting and respectful relationship.

Key # 179 - The destination of our life's journey is wisely kept well hidden within us: it's up to us to discover it!

As our journey develops creatively, we sail through it in joy, commandeered by our divine light within. This comfort delivers the peace of mind we seek.

The process of fulfillment requires a look at the relationship we have with ourselves. In Chapter 9 we discussed this. How do you treat yourself?

Key # 180 - It is the little things that go undetected that we must become keenly aware of.

You will never be able to accept a compliment that you cannot give to yourself. When you are the captain of your ship, you are "in charge" of designing your destiny. Do you want it to be fun, or depressing? A silly question, right? Adopt the attitude that you are on a journey of ultimate joy and you will have a journey of joy. Adopt the attitude that you want your experiences to deliver only wisdom to make the next step more accurately, opening to even greater possibilities.

Key # 181 - Some voyages may seem more challenging than others.

They may take you up a steep mountain or along treacherous paths. When you arrive, however, you will have reached a higher perspective. You will breathe in the freshness of mountain air or the tranquility of a deep forest.

Some of our journeys take us through valleys of deep emotions where we gather strength for our next ascent that could mean climbing cliffs of rugged challenges—for the sake of adventure and accomplishment. Ah! The delight of a journey; the restfulness of a pause.

Other adventures take us on a roller-coaster ride for the mere thrill of the adventure. When you were younger, do you remember your own awesome thrust into life? Or the child-like trust of a happy moment?

Key # 182 - The beauty of life lies in the fact that everything reveals itself in time.

Some journeys take us into long drawn-out adventures of pain and suffering, but only because we have been unaware of our great power within. Others deliver us up into a mound of difficulties simply to challenge us into discovering our greater strengths.

Sometimes we are blind to our own amazing discoveries. We do not see the pearls of wisdom which lie before our eyes. If you find that you often call yourself "impatient," look deeper into your issues of "control."

Involve yourself in other activities, such as service projects: volunteer work or playing with small children. When we find ourselves in temporary blindness we can gain a moment of reprieve while in these activities. Have you ever noticed how much faster the week goes when you have a great adventurous plan for the weekend? Is it that, feeling the adventure, we tend to get excited and want to participate in it ahead of time?

Key # 183 - *The world is viewed as the observer desires.*

And who might the observer be? None other than ourselves. It has been well documented that as we think so we become. While on this journey of life, we often come to a place where we must reflect and ask ourselves about our purpose in living the life in which we are presently engaged (which is the result of what we have been thinking and creating).

We often find ourselves not knowing what it is that we want. *This is the point of power, the present moment,* so we must ease ourselves through the "bottle neck" by writing down our thoughts.

Through the writing, our subconscious mind is letting us know what it is that we want. Here is where your inner wisdom, the power within, will now ask: "*Why does it make a difference whether or not I achieve this goal?*"

The answer you now come up with will become a key to the direction you will follow.

In her book, *Write It Down, Make It Happen*, Henriette Anne Klauser, Ph.D. stated, "Putting it on paper alerts the part of your brain known as the reticular activating system to join in the play." It is extremely important to keep your journal updated with your ideas, dreams, meditations, inspirations and other messages.

Erwin Schroedinger, an Austrian physicist, proved with his famous Schroedinger's cat experiment, that the observer determines whether the experimental cat is discovered dead or alive inside the cage.

A cat is placed inside a steel cage containing one radioactive atom having what is called a "half-life" of one hour (which indicates that in a sample of material containing such atoms, only half of them would remain active after the passing of one hour). After the passing of one hour (when the cat is placed in the cage) the chances of finding the atom intact, still capable of activating the photocell in the cage, are 50–50.

In this cage is a sensitive photocell that when activated by this single atom will release a poisonous gas that will kill Schrodinger's cat. Thus, after one hour we have two possibilities: finding the cat dead or the cat alive, depending whether or not the photocell has been activated, prior to the cat being placed in the cage. [For additional information, see *Taking The Quantum Leap*, by physicist, Fred Allan Wolf, page 190.]

Who controls the fate of the cat? Schrodinger and quantum mechanics answers: the observer.

Change is Natural

Key # 184 - Change is a natural evolutionary process that brings one to self-fulfillment.

In this evolutionary process of development we perceive new ideas and embark on fresh adventures, based on our focus on those ideas. We travel into new avenues of life and discover not only new horizons but an unlimited amount of possibilities!

Many people are more naturally geared toward visual thinking. The verbal-linear process imposed upon us by our school systems and our social norms have impaired this natural visual thinking mode.

Gratitude is Magical

Key # 185 - The power of gratitude is magical.

When we have gratitude for the results desired before they are realized, we formulate their quickening into our reality. Knowing, (not simply believing) that our dreams are near, subtly delivers the reality of these dreams, almost as if you were watching a scene appear in a movie right before your eyes.

Focus on Finish—as if already done. Have you ever noticed how we have a habit of making "to do" lists? Instead, we need to get into the habit of making "done" lists.

Amanda, one of the most pleasant clients of mine, shared a beautiful story with me about abundance in her life. Amanda lived in a small community in the mountains; she had a beautiful log cabin with a fireplace in the middle of the main front room. Two other rooms provided the necessary living quarters that Amanda desired for her comfortable existence.

I met Amanda in the town's grocery store. We seemed to run into each other often, so one day we decided to have coffee together. Soon I discovered she was a person who had found fulfillment in the simple life. She had an abundant, resourceful and wise outlook. Amanda never condemned, criticized or complained about anyone or anything. She had only positive words to say about all of her life's experiences. "If you ever find yourself where you think you were wrong," she whispered, "admit it quickly and emphatically, then let it go; this will bring to you peace of mind."

I internalized her statement and responded, "What a beautiful way to look at those sneaky thoughts that sometimes slip into our minds. Abundance can come to us if we accept the thought that mistakes are simple steps to getting us where we want to go ... then continue on with our discovery of the richness that life has to offer—regardless of the simplicity of our existence."

Once you attain the ability to have a deliberate route to your happiness because you know you are the creator of your own destiny, you experience peaceful moments more often.

Marlene, another loyal client of mine, one day related how she loved the changes she had recently made in her life. "I came to realize that all I had to do to be happy was to commit to deliberately choosing only what I preferred."

"You make it sound like a recent discovery," I said.

"Yes, it was something I just noticed that really made a difference in my life, so 'Bingo!' I quickly adopted it as a part of my life." Marlene was proud and pleased with herself.

Having the ability to design your life when you know it is a journey and not a destination allows you to pace yourself as you desire, and to enjoy the momentum of your own creations.

Self-Fulfillment Brings Strength

Key # 186 - Self-fulfillment comes decorated with strength of character.

Ever wonder why? Consider the story of the mouse who took on the challenge of removing a splinter from a lion's paw. This little mouse must have been well on his way to self-fulfillment. Had he been weak of character he certainly would have refused to help the lion.

Lions are mortal enemies to mice! Yes, if this little mouse had relied on traditional thinking, he would have been too frightened to help the lion. Instead, he challenged his strength of character to the max—and what was the result of his act? You know the rest of that story.

Key # 187 - On our life's journey into forever, we are only voyagers.

Self-value is just that: having value in what we represent for ourselves. On this journey we decide by our own actions how we are to finish. We make choices along the way of how we are going to live our life and how we are going to relate to others. If self-fulfillment is what we wish for ourselves, then our thoughts, words and actions will support that destiny.

Rex, one of my most interesting clients commented on his self-fulfilling prophecy: "I never was so surprised about the truth of one's values until I plunged into my own fears with deliberate passion," said Rex, grinning broadly.

"Ah, so what does that mean?" I asked.

"I was in the middle of a heated conversation with a friend and he insinuated that I had lied to him. I resented this assumption and took it personally. But upon my instant review of my own reaction, I decided to show my strength of character rather than my strength in body and told him that as long as he would believe this, he would destroy our friendship. I was not going to stand for the accusation." Rex beamed proudly as he related his story.

"Because the theater of your mind is a place where you can practice perfectly each and every time, your mental exercise is the use of visualization to rehearse a successful performance or behavior," I reminded him. "You are powerful! Give yourself a big pat on the back." I patted him on his shoulder and finished his haircut.

"Thanks," he said, "I look as great as I feel now!"

Having an open mind to unsuspecting outcomes re-enforces self-worth.

Consider Your Integrity

Key # 188 - Our integrity is the way we see ourselves as part of the whole picture.

Like the carpet installer who uses a chalk line on the jute back-side of the carpet to mark the smaller cuts from the large roll, we too can have a code to follow if we are to practice what we say we stand for. Become familiar with your code of behavior and practice it daily.

Carlee, one of the high school girls who came in to see me monthly for a haircut, recognized the importance of being certain of one's values. "Do you think it's good to talk with your friends about the most important traits we wish to adopt in our life?" Carlee asked, looking at a hairstyle book and tilting her head to listen intently to my answer.

"I certainly do!" I responded. "Do you feel it is?"

"Oh, I thought it was. That was why I asked. I have a very good friend who always listens to me and has valuable input to my comments."

I thought it curious to hear such a comment from a youngster.

She continued, "I trust your opinion, that's why I asked you. You've always given me good advice, so I wanted to hear your opinion, that's all." She looked at herself in the mirror and smiled.

"I'm proud of you, Carlee," I said. "You are very wise."

"Integrity" is the silent middle name of a master. Other forms of the word are 'integrate' and 'integral', which denote a quality of character that is fundamental to the making of a master—the amalgamation of virtues which describe the incorruptibility of a person. This is becoming an "integral" part of the whole picture—becoming complete!

Appreciate Your Own Usefulness

Key # 189 - Self-appreciation for the resource we can be to others is valuable.

Do you know how to appreciate your own usefulness? Here are some interesting questions to ask yourself:

- Do I feel I can be helpful to others?
- Do I accept comments from others that describe how they feel I am valuable to them in their life?
- Do I feel highly valuable in relationships, thus registering high self-esteem?
- Can I think of creative or practical ideas to contribute to someone else's situations?

Patricia, a friend of mine, complements my life with her courage and strength. She shows me she has worth by the service she is willing to share with me. She has a busy life, yet she takes the time to help me with tasks that require a long time for me to complete. She is very willing to give of her self, demonstrating to her friends her love for them.

"The load of tomorrow, added to that of yesterday, carried today, makes the strongest falter. We must learn to shut out the future as tightly as the past," said Sir William Osler. Being a truth seeker is an unending task because there is no place to stop and camp.

Key # 190 - Once you open the channels of your own understanding, you too will feel the rapture of being alive.

Many years ago my friend Tom enlightened me to my own lack of self-understanding. He told me that most of us say that what we're seeking is a meaning for life. We discussed this often and came to the conclusion that what we are all seeking has more to do with an experience of being alive than with the search for the meaning of life.

For him it seemed simple to say, but for me, at that time, it was difficult to comprehend. Later, as I grew in understanding, we came to agree on the fact that life experiences bring us to knowing our innermost being, our self-worth.

Tom had a way of leaving things alone and telling me that time would come to bear its truth. And again, sure enough, that is what happened. I recognized that my refusal at times to change was nothing more than my devotion to ignorance; not allowing myself to discover new horizons.

By following principles of self-fulfillment and applying their secrets, I generated a feeling of serenity. I came to understand the meaning of my experiences and the "moral of the story" of my life as it developed right before my eyes. Life became like a vacation on a house boat. I was basking in the sun, sharing precious time with wonderful friends and drinking cool refreshing drinks.

Key # 191 - Knowing that life is a process and not a destination, will afford the peace and happiness that comes from self-acceptance.

Robert Louis Stevenson put it perfectly: "To be what we are, and to become what we are capable of becoming is the only end of life."

Life experiences bring us to knowing our innermost being, the divine within—our self-worth. Lack of self-worth is the acceptance of incompleteness; it is ignorance of the virtue of allowing life to be a journey and not making it into a destination.

Often it is difficult to comprehend these concepts. Only when you come to understand yourself can you come to know yourself.

Have a Feather-Light Heart

Having a light heart makes room for new and fulfilling experiences. Here are six steps to experiencing a self-fulfilling and joyful life:

1. Enjoy the simple and beautiful things of life.
2. Exude your own fragrance—your personal gift to life, and add to the bouquet of creation. Harmonize with all of life.
3. Be more conscious of your neighbors. Become aware of their energy. The proximity of any energy will eventually synergize with yours and create its own experience.
4. Select your experiences carefully. Every experience is just one of unlimited possibilities brought into reality.
5. Create only what you prefer to realize—take an attitude of adventure.
6. Connect with the Universal Mind consciously. It delivers the support for your dreams to come true.

The moment one definitely commits oneself, then providence moves too. All sorts of things occur to help one that would never otherwise have occurred. A whole stream of events issues from the decision, raising in one's favor all manner of unforeseen incidents and meetings and material assistance, which no man could have dreamed would have come his way.

— W. H. Murray

Key # 192 - To desire a spontaneous result is nothing more than living the natural impulse to create self-fulfillment.

Socrates said: "I believe we cannot live better than in seeking to become still better than we are." This is the nature of our existence; to seek fulfillment and to involve ourselves in the unknown.

Love is a Virtue, Not an Emotion

Key # 193 - Love is who we are!

Love is the virtue of being self-fulfilled. Love is about being-ness—not restricting our natural expression. It is about doing-ness—expressing our sincere creative nature in all experiences. And it is about having-ness—owning what we bring into creation by the nature of our being-ness.

The common and accepted concept says we must have, before we can do anything or before we can be anyone. But in actuality, we must *be* first, so that we can do; and once we *are* love, we can have anything we want!

If we do it in reverse—having-ness, doing-ness and then being-ness we will find ourselves on the sacrificial altar of self-sabotage and in the lack/loss/limitation syndrome.

When we are who we are first, the magic will follow. We will be doing what we love, which will come naturally. This, in turn, will produce the having-ness that will fulfill our life.

Tracking Questions

1. What may you be prompted to do if you were to act as an over-achiever?
2. Have you ever experienced becoming a butterfly after having been a caterpillar? If so, how did you feel?
3. What statement would you use to describe your life: "half full" or "half empty"?
4. What character attitudes may you acquire in your life to attain self-fulfillment?

5. Pretend you are self-fulfilled. How does this feel?
6. Are you seeking for a meaning in life or for the experience of being alive? Explain.

Tracking Exercises

1. Write a paragraph that describes you as a highly motivated and creative individual.
2. Take a sheet of paper and draw and color a picture of your idea of a feather-light heart.
3. List ten beautiful virtues that exist in your character today.
4. Finish this statement: I know myself because I can say I am _____.
5. Describe how you feel about "being-ness," "doing-ness" and "having-ness."
6. What one thing would you say you find yourself devoted to that has kept you in ignorance?

Conclusion

"All knowledge is but remembrance."

— Plato

Is it ordinary life or extraordinary life that you want? Does the information contained in this book truly make you remember something you already knew? Does this knowledge bring you to remembrance?

"There is no such thing as chance; and what to us seems merest accident springs from the deepest source of destiny," writes Johann Christoph Friedrich in *The Death of Wallenstein*. Are you perhaps reaching into your destiny by reading this book? Is mastership of life part of the destiny you have chosen? Are you ready to call yourself a master? Did you acquire the self-worth you sought by reading this book? What are you going to do with all of this information you've gathered? What does it really mean? What does it really matter to have all this stuff running through your brain? Is it just one more book under your belt?

Each of us must answer these questions individually; and hopefully end up with a jeweled master's diadem, where knowledge is treasured as wisdom, remembrance is brought to the forefront and ignorance is abolished.

It is not a coincidence that great minds in history have been moved to do their purposeful work through a desire to vanquish ignorance—to cast a light upon humanity and bring knowledge to the world. I've often pondered the words of Socrates: "There is only one good—knowledge; and one evil—ignorance." Paramahansa Yogananda, another great wise man from India, said: "Ignorance is the supreme disease."

One Last Bit of Wisdom

We encourage the acquiring of more knowledge because it gives us greater ability to solve problems. Problem—or riddle-solving challenges the spirit to grow by exercising its creative imagination.

As a child, I eagerly looked forward to Saturdays when my father's friend and neighbor, Rene Bouscayrol would come over to visit the rubber plantation where we lived, in the outskirts of the Guatemalan tropical jungle. He always challenged me with an interesting riddle. Every week I'd mentally work to solve the new puzzle in order to present it to my mentor the following week.

We can perceive the labyrinth of life as difficult. We can also see life's challenges as interesting opportunities for growth. If we capture the eagerness and excitement of a child, the labyrinth will seem like a game. The challenge will be fun and we will welcome the opportunity to grow.

Benjamin Franklin said: "Those things that hurt, instruct." It's true; often we feel overwhelmed by difficult challenges; we feel as though we have failed. But once we understand that we have the power to meet and overcome these challenges, the sting disappears. Through our creative imagination we realize the solution lies with the acquisition of more knowledge.

Gather Some Tools

Let the words in this book be your tools. Integrate them into your life. Use them. Feel them. Experience, or live them. Become the child eager to solve the riddles of life, and just as eager to share your solutions with others.

Prejudice Joins Hands with Ignorance

Prejudice and ignorance are two monsters you do not want to welcome into your life. Sometimes, however, like stray neighborhood cats they may end up in your back yard. Getting rid of these pests can be challenging.

Accept the challenge. Shine the light of knowledge on yourself by asking questions, being curious and eager to learn, and unwilling to take others' opinions at face value. Do your own research. Making a conscious effort to shine the light of knowledge on whatever you do not know or want to know more about, leads to enlightenment.

Learn from your experience. Apply your knowledge ... and acknowledge your inner desire to grow—to be and do and know more about ourselves and life. This wizard within is our inner spark of the divine.

Sir Thomas Browne said: "Life is a pure flame, and we live by an invisible sun within us."

Like Socrates, I call ignorance evil, only because it limits our ability to make wiser choices in life and not because I pass judgment upon those who are unaware. Yet prejudice, the twin sister to ignorance, can be more ferocious because it is a conscious coveting of our own explanations or beliefs. We hold onto them tightly and do not allow new information to enter.

Wisdom from Great Minds

The Nobel Prize in literature was awarded to the poet, Bengal Rabindranath Tagore for his beautiful words of inspiration. Here is one of my favorite Tagore poems: "True education is not pumped and crammed in from outward sources, but aids in bringing to the surface the infinite hoard of wisdom within."

From Mabel Collins, in her book, *The Idyll Of The White Lotus* (1884), are other words of wisdom: "The principle which gives life dwells in us and without us, is undying and beneficent, is not heard or seen or smelt, but it is perceived by the man who desires perception."

The evolution of this perception is a personal quest for knowledge. This search for knowledge in life sometimes appears as a mystery, a labyrinth each of us must work through in order to "unravel" our path and "travel" forward.

We must each come to understand that every opportunity we create for ourselves is an exercise in knowledge. Reading this book is one more effort to gain knowledge, one step closer to remembering. With knowledge we will exercise greater skill in self-preservation and forward movement—evolution.

The philosopher Frederick Nietzsche, in *Beyond Good and Evil*, said: "A living thing seeks above all to discharge its strength—life itself, its will to power ... self preservation is only one of the direct and most frequent results." The scientist Pierre Teilhard de Chardin called this search for knowledge "Law of Complexity-Consciousness." Chardin wrote: "Evolution proceeds in the direction of increasing complexity which is accompanied by a corresponding rise in consciousness."

Survival is not the only force that causes evolution in a being. Consciousness evolves through developing more awareness. Our personal evolution is the evolution of the community as a whole—the attainment of oneness.

Perhaps you have already realized that all things end in mystery before we come to know. It is our own discovery of life in knowledge—in awareness that begins to resolve that mystery. The great inventor Marconi said: "The mystery of life is certainly the most persistent problem ever placed before the thought of man." He too felt compelled to evolve humanity by contributing his wisdom.

By communicating with each other and sharing information, we come to a state of oneness. Then we function as a coherent unique mechanism moving toward the same end, allowing us to evolve together.

Waking Up

Through the insights shared in this book, we will discover if we haven't already, that most of our answers lie within. Although nature brings us the gift of life, knowledge plus experience equaling wisdom, enhances that life, making it more beautiful ... and meaningful. As we discover the truth of our own nature— the wizard within—we can learn to love ourselves and develop into masters.

You may have thought that all of these life secrets I'm sharing with you were hidden from you only because your eyes were not open to them. In reality, they have always been evident in your life. The consciousness was not there yet to perceive them, to bring them into focus.

Again, Marcel Proust said: "The real journey of discovery consists not in seeking new landscapes but in having new eyes." Once you have lived these secrets of ancient wisdom, you will be able to create your own world of self-designed dreams.

Sri Yukteswar, a highly revered guru from India, has an empowering way of describing wisdom as "not assimilated with the eyes but with the atoms. When your conviction of truth is not merely in your brain but in your being, you may differently vouch for its meaning."

As you begin to use the concepts outlined in this book, you will start to perceive more clearly that knowledge comes sufficiently equipped to destroy ignorance and prejudice.

Knowledge cannot spring from any other source than self-discovery of who we truly are and then, seeking within for our answers.

Meditation rituals alone will not abolish ignorance and prejudice. Meditating yourself into a paradise has its merits, but this is not what I am advocating. You must live life happily, in relationship with others. This is why service is so fulfilling.

Ponder upon the principles in this book until they become integrated into your self. The purpose of this book is to help you extract your wisdom within and to assist in the process of integrating this wisdom.

The information I have shared from my life's experiences is to serve as an example—a point of reference as the first step for you to launch your own journey. It is my hope that you gain trust in yourself to know that you can come to integrate your physical, mental, emotional, psychical and spiritual feelings.

When we dedicate our life to living it fully, we dedicate it to answering the question: "Who am I?" We integrate our life with others instead of hiding behind a mask. It is my hope that all of us will passionately and freely live in the light of the wisdom extracted from our experiences. We will then walk in enlightenment with our chin up!

Experiences we create surely teach us there is a small but important difference between keeping your chin up and sticking your neck out. Ignorance causes us to stick out our necks; knowledge of who we are, assists us in keeping our chin up.

Know Thyself and to Thine Own Self Be True

Let's press on, always true to our selves, confronting our weaknesses and sailing through our journey in delight.

A spiritual journey should go hand in hand with the introspection and self-analysis which I encourage in this book. It should accompany the effort to track self-worth.

The wise person travels to discover themselves; they make life a journey of transformation. It is through our conscious and deliberately chosen practical efforts that we cultivate a feather-light heart that delivers a life that will not deliver unfortunate consequences. Then, ultimately, death becomes only a surmountable transformation.

A Great Discovery

It was through my experiences, seriously appreciating them, that I discovered my "I am." This realization, which I call my truth, came unexpectedly.

First, I earnestly put myself on the path for discovering my own truth (turning inward) rather than walking into the wild world of the unknown (turning outward).

Second, I accepted that truth in loving grace (turning inward).

Finally, I reached out to share with others what I had discovered (turning outward).

This is what you will find yourself doing … guaranteed! I've witnessed this amazing transformation many times, with those who have sincerely wanted to become masters of their life.

It really does not matter where you are now. You will be exactly at the right place and time to begin your transformation. Clearly recognize and appreciate all you have experienced up to now, regardless of how unfair or terrible it may have seemed. Do not have any expectations; accept your own "truth" as it will come. The more I had preconceived ideas as to how it "should" be happening, the more it eluded me.

I soon discovered that the most joyous experience is lived in the moment. Transformation came when I had a stunning realization of my own truth—enlightenment about who I really am—my truth! It indeed inspires a holy confidence, as expressed by the Indian Master Yukteswar. You too will realize some day that all along there was something special, something tremendous within you, that for some reason had eluded you.

Do not be dismayed by the wonderment you will carry with you. You will also carry this awe or wonderment in your heart. It is this expectancy that will thrust you into the unknown.

In *Living In The Light*, Shakti Gawain & Laurel King describe this expectancy: "As each of us connects with our inner spiritual awareness, we learn that the creative power of the universe is within us. We also learn that we can create our own reality and take responsibility for doing so. The change begins within each individual, but as more and more individuals are transformed, the mass consciousness is increasingly affected."

Our old path is not leading us to feelings of deep fulfillment, satisfaction, and joy. We need to find a new path ... and
the direction or flow is "inward to outward."

Finally Living Our Vision

Spiritual evolution is what life is all about. In our life, our
vision is who we are, what we represent, and what we are
bringing about or creating. Discovering our world as an adventure of life is called "living our vision." It is the way we explore
the realms of the unknown and make them a part of our experiences—owning them, loving them and gaining wisdom from
them.

When we live our vision, we are moving forward; we are
not repeating the same story with different characters. Simply
desiring to have, be or do is not the action of accomplishing. It
takes *will* to bring about an action; and it takes passion.

Once you establish a vision with passion, your will propels
the desire. Your vision is what inspires; your desire is what
expires the vision and makes it transpire. Let's now apply what
we've learned in this book and share it with others. Begin to
feel it!

Noble on the Wave of Happiness

Being able to be happy today is the real proof of success. The
cure for boredom is not diversion. The cure for boredom is to
find some work to do, something to care about—to have passion for. Lethargy is another worm that hates the light, because
it doesn't let you apply what you know. Don't be afraid to
touch the divine in your life. Be certain that this knowledge is
not purely intellectual.

The power within you comes to bear its fruit by your
constant application of the principles for which you stand.
When you implement knowledge with experience you gather

flowers of happiness and fruits of wisdom. This requires physical participation and interaction with others. It means experiencing your life, not merely thinking it will come to fruition. You must put action into your thoughts. Make action an integrated part of your life. Seclusion, cloistering oneself, does not bring happiness. It is integration and love for all in service that bring about the delight of life.

As you share with others what you have read here, you will imprint these principles permanently and consciously in your own mind. Refer to these "keys" often. They will be the guideposts on your path. The joy of sharing with others is an added gift; you will soon well understand.

If you are still "wanting," this is an indication that you are unfulfilled—that you have a desire for yet something else. The trick is to be in bliss "knowing" that "all" can be yours at your simplest arousal of desire for it. Learn to be satisfied with this knowing until the dream materializes.

When you feel unfulfilled, you have a sense of unhappiness which in turn will plague you and cause your mental processes to initiate a condition of emotions that begins to unconsciously destroy your dream. This is yet another worm that eats away at your enthusiasm and self-worth.

The "good life" means appreciating our successes, living passionately for today and purposefully for tomorrow. "Noble" means loving who and what you are right now, because you know the process of passionately desiring more, is going to take you on an unlimited adventure that will be exciting beyond your wildest dreams.

"Noble" is the attitude in which one holds oneself. Nobility never compares. Don't be a prisoner of the past. In India small elephants' ankles are tied up with a chain attached to a post. They grow up learning to remain tied to the post. When they grow older they only need to be tied to a small twig by a string and they do not escape. Their memory has made an imprint from the past and has made them slaves to their past.

We need to let go of the past and move on. Don't be prejudiced and close your mind to new ideas from others by holding on too tightly to your own.

Establish Your Own Code

Scientists continue to search for a standard or mean measurement that will give them a basis or code for their experiments. In contrast to this qualified and accepted professional method, I have used "myself" as that measurement. I have been my own guinea pig. Throughout my life I have used my own results as my code. This code and my own acquired "truth" from living concepts of ancient wisdom, are what I have shared with you in this book.

What you have read in these pages are experiences of my personal life—my conscious observation of my own experiences as a consciousness (that inner light) within a human body. I've taken full responsibility of what I have experienced through life. This means I am conscious of the fact that I manifest my outcomes.

Review and Review

With each re-reading of this book, the concepts will leave a deeper impression. It has been my experience that if I read a book a second or even third time, I begin to approach the contents with the same mind as the author. This procedure has been a great asset in my life. By having a better idea of what the author has in mind, I can more readily grasp both the information as well as the intent, and thus integrate with the spirit in which it was written. Here is the formula I use:

1. I read over the entire book once at normal speed to grasp its main idea.
2. I absorb only what I can.

3. I begin to read it a second time slowly, this time paragraph by paragraph, pausing as often as I need to extract meaning.

4. I pay deep attention to subject matter; I think through what I'm learning.

5. If the book provides questions and tracking exercises, I work through them, giving myself a good mental work-out.

6. After reading the book carefully a second time and completing the work at the end of each chapter, I meditate about what I have learned.

7. Sometimes I may find my mind wandering, but I know this is normal.

8. I contemplate each thought that comes to me.

9. Before rushing into the next thought, I write down in my journal my understanding of that thought.

10. Finally—the most important step—I review each thought and see myself living each concept as I've understood it.

It is not what you read that can give you freedom, growth and joy, but what you do with what you read. Once you have read this book, you may have acquainted yourself with the contents, but its teachings are still raw material. They will remain only that, like tools unused, until you put these teachings or concepts to work in your life.

Apply the concepts in this book to your daily experiences. To read and not realize or apply the philosophy is like the old Dutchman's donkey that carries the gold out of the Superstition mountain on his back and never is able to know its value.

If you follow this procedure of reading, re-reading, doing the exercises, absorbing and meditating on the concepts and teachings ... then applying them, you will be surprised how the quality of your life will start to improve.

Go over the questions and exercises at the end of each chapter and review your progress. The feeling of accomplishment you will experience will be magical. Repeat this process a year later, and again re-experience the thrill!

Know this for certain: There is only one program: "I AM." All else is enfolded within this knowledge. "As conscious beings the only thing we need to find happiness in life is to perceive clearly who we are ..." says Ken Keyes in his book, *Handbook Of Higher Consciousness*, "... but to achieve this clear perception of ourselves and the world around us takes constant inner work."

I call this book a golden four-faceted key for opening a door to another dimension of our existence.

The four facets are:

1. Love: that feeling that simply oozes out of your soul (without the chemical/hormonal trigger) and bathes your entire body with peace.
2. Humility: complete relaxing of all self-imposed chemical/sensual emotions.
3. Expectancy: the awe and wonderment for things unknown.
4. Lightness of heart: a feeling that uplifts you to the pinnacle of your existence.

Just as in quantum physics, perception is altered by concentration on the focused thought of a particular outcome, you will need to gather all that constitutes the four facets of this key in order to "switch into" a parallel universe. If any of the facets are missing, the key will not work.

Self-worth cannot be bought in the marketplace; it cannot be swallowed in a capsule or pill and realized by ingestion. Self-worth must be earnestly sought through daily application of sound principles and deliberate, conscious changes that you make. These changes are based on self-realized principles of your truth and purpose for life. The rewards are happiness and a spiritual awakening that brings forth the light within as a guide to your life. This guide will keep you focused on your goal or destiny.

May this book be a window through which you see the face of god—your inner light. May it be a joy that awakens enthusiasm, determination, clarity, creativity, calmness, abundant health and subtle peace. May it also be a friend to you, one who will see your already lived experiences as stepping-stones to where you are today.

Tune into the Cosmic Consciousness and fly with the eagles! Become an artist at living your life as designed by your inner light.

Have your life be your work of art. Live the moment! Seize the moment! Live in the light of your Highest Consciousness.

Your castle is now ready to be lived in!!!

The true purpose of life lies in being who you are. And who are you? LOVE! Bon Voyage!

And ... don't hesitate to contact me at Mind & Body Works, 107 W. Wade Lane, Ste. 3, Payson, AZ 85541. My e-mail address is: azodonnal@npgcable.com.

Appendix

Keys for Tracking Your Self-Worth

Key # 1 - The way out of where you find yourself today is through the same door that brought you here.

Key # 2 - Experience teaches in a lifetime what passion can teach in an hour.

Key # 3 - Focus on the joy you are attempting to achieve and the self-gratifying reward will be happiness.

Key # 4 - The magical door to self-discovery is not outside somewhere, but "within."

Key # 5 - Self-healing can easily be achieved through the power of forgiveness.

Key # 6 - Forgiveness is the key to freedom, joy and self-love.

Key # 7 - Keeping life simple can be effortless.

Key # 8 - Letting go of the past refreshes the present moment.

Key # 9 - Acting as if, even if it is not actually so, brings results in time.

Key # 10 - How you feel about yourself is how you will appear to others.

Key # 11 - Enthusiasm gives you the perspective necessary to reach a balance.

Key # 12 - Seeing it in your mind is like having it!

Key # 13 - Being certain about what you want creates the energy to materialize it.

Key # 14 - In order to be successful, you must first give yourself permission to use this freedom.

Key # 15 - Worry is a nasty worm that thrives on enthusiasm.

Key # 16 - It's the little things that count.

Key # 17 - Your limitations are only what you believe them to be.

Key # 18 - Feeling great every moment keeps you centered.

Key # 19 - When you are happy with yourself it is easy to be happy with others.

Key # 20 - Know that you are free to create the world you wish to experience.

Key # 21 - Your outcomes will match your attitudes.

Key # 22 - Manifested life is a fallout of our thinking.

Key # 23 - When fears are on the rampage we create more of what we fear.

Key # 24 - Transparent beliefs are bearers of unhappiness.

Key # 25 - If you free your life of emotional obstacles you will make room for accomplishments.

Key # 26 - Some situations rob you of your calm; neutralize them.

Key # 27 - Once you release the past and allow the present to spearhead the future, trusting in the divine power within, you will evolve much faster.

Key # 28 - Changing your mind is not a problem; so, stop punishing yourself for doing it.

Key #29 - Avoidance is an indication that other people usually have something to do with your indecision.

Key # 30 - When you are able to hold a dream—a passionate desire—in focus, it is easier for the universal forces to deliver what you desire.

Key # 31 - Living "as if" is truly living the magic of your power within.

Key # 32 - Strong feelings are the key to manifesting your dreams.

Key # 33 - Evaluating your progress after initial application of an idea is imperative to the establishing of a habit.

Key # 34 - If we are to change outcomes we must also replace established attitudes with those we have determined are ready to supply the energy we are after.

Key # 35 - Experiences take you where you want to go.

Key # 36 - Conversations and relationships are a result of our thinking.

Key # 37 - Your words are the building blocks to your experiences.

Key # 38 - If a thought can cause an intention, a thought can also turn it around.

Key # 39 - Becoming passionate about the outcome of our life causes us to develop more creative ways to relate to others.

Key # 40 - One of the most common stumbling blocks to a simple and blissful life is the conditioned belief in time as a reality.

Key # 41 - It is not necessary to defend your point of view.

Key # 42 - Sound decisions bring happiness and self-satisfaction; they bring peace of mind and a healthy outlook on life.

Key # 43 - When we have sufficient knowledge about the direction we intend to follow, we can proceed with wise choices and enjoy the outcome.

Key # 44 - The power behind that moment in which you make your decision is integrally related to knowing you are accountable for your choices.

Key # 45 - Know full well if your choices are influenced by others.

Key # 46 - Surround yourself with successful people whose ideas have led them to achieve their goals.

Key # 47 - What you presently value highly has a lot to do with the way you have experienced your relationships with people, places, things and situations in the past.

Key # 48 - Our behaviors and outcomes are strongly influenced by our decision to imitate or reject our parents' values.

Key # 49 - The need for peer pressure will disappear as we emerge with our own agendas, our own destinies.

Key # 50 - Determine if you prefer to experience something different and do so without feelings of guilt.

Key # 51 - There is a way to redeem yourself and gain strength from a decision you wish to abandon.

Key # 52 - When you have established strong skills for making decisions, based on knowing your values, the actual process for taking action is easier.

Key # 53 - Before you begin to consider what decision best fits you, first it is important to identify your values.

Key # 54 - When facing a decision, make sure you come equipped with your values in order!

Key # 55 - When necessary, take time to seek counsel from professionals before making your decision.

Key # 56 - If you made a decision that produced undesirable or unwanted consequences, don't let this single experience destroy your life forever!

Key # 57 - Don't allow discouragement to deplete your precious energy.

Key # 58 - Once you have become comfortable with what is most important to you, decisions come quickly.

Key # 59 - Making our own choices is a natural and enriching ability when we are prepared to use our innateness.

Key # 60 - Your signs of transformation will include your ability to have a more positive outlook.

Key # 61 - Monitoring your changes is one of the most valuable aspects of your journey.

Key # 62 - Commitment and dedication to personal improvement are part of developing our character and establishing a strong and firm foundation for excellence in life.

Key # 63 - "Quality" refers to choices you or others have made that are based on a set of values.

Key # 64 - Practice leads to improvement!

Key # 65 - Experiences involve relationships with others, yourself or nature.

Key # 66 - Life created intentionally implies a will to be involved in the adventure.

Key # 67 - Wisdom comes as a result of having taken the risk into the unknown to recover the truth of your being.

Key # 68 - Harmony is the twin sibling of balance.

Key # 69 - To add quality to your life, you will be learning about people, places and cultures.

Key # 70 - When we refrain from meddling with people, they seem to take care of themselves.

Key # 71 - Life is a process; journeying toward our dreams is a process.

Key # 72 - Quality of life does not mean equality.

Key # 73 - Competition can destroy the pure intent of any event.

Key # 74 - Excellence comes as a gift when specializing in your field of endeavor.

Key # 75 - Experiencing the senses and responding to them awakens your passion for life.

Key # 76 - The circumstances and relationships you encounter reward you with knowledge about yourself.

Key # 77 - The passion-filled thrust we give to every involvement is the deliberate and intentional living of our dream.

Key # 78 - If you experience doubt at any time, recall your successes.

Key # 79 - The best way to understand the language of your inner self is to start paying attention to messages from your physical body.

Key # 80 - The process of meditation is one of the oldest and most effective ways to access guidance from our subconscious mind, and thus re-program our thought process.

Key # 81 - When you "go within," you will find the real power behind the entire process of manifesting your self-worth and a quality life.

Key # 82 - The art of being conscious—concentrating and paying attention—begins in daily life.

Key # 83 - Entering this sacred silence through meditation is the beginning of being able to communicate with the Self—the subconscious mind.

Key # 84 - Contemplation is the key to meditation.

Key # 85 - When we become consciously aware of our emotions without judgment we experience true love for ourselves and others.

Key # 86 - Judgment separates; discernment includes.

Key # 87 - In a state of open-mindedness we can become tolerant of viewpoints and activities of others that may seem abusive and destructive.

Key # 88 - A grateful heart is a peaceful one.

Key # 89 - Search for a source of self-knowledge outside ourselves only prolongs the process of growth.

Key # 90 - Combined daily activity and meditation, will deliver the quality life you are looking for.

Key # 91 - Letting go of these attitudes will require a firm and steady commitment to taking time for solitude and introspection.

Key # 92 - Most of the patterns of behavior that are no longer useful have a built-in self-sabotaging mechanism.

Key # 93 - In the process of switching from one frame of reference to another, you will find yourself dealing with your ego.

Key # 94 - Hidden agendas in any relationship eventually deliver pain.

Key # 95 - Closing the door on the excitement of life is an indication that your energy is stuck in the disappointments of the past.

Key # 96 - If you can remember that everything you experience in your life you have personally created, you will be more understanding and forgiving of yourself.

Key # 97 - Your viewpoints and preference for doing things a certain way, will be two of the most difficult "attachments" to release.

Key # 98 - Detaching from the need to have things work out in a certain way—"your way"—indicates progress in your stability of living in the present moment.

Key # 99 - Willingness to detach from what others think of you is another indication of coming in contact with your own true self-image.

Key # 100 - If you find yourself associating regularly with those who are attached to other people's opinions and you base some of your actions and decisions on their approval or validation, this is an indication of your own attachment to others' opinions.

Key # 101 - Removing yourself from other people's dramas and issues does not mean that you don't care.

Key # 102 - Becoming detached will give you freedom and energy you never dreamed could be yours.

Key # 103 - It is the act of letting go, that crowns your attitude of trust.

Key # 104 - Strength comes in knowing you are not affected by others.

Key # 105 - Engaging in a hobby is a way of keeping yourself happy.

Key # 106 - We establish neural-net connections through repeated patterns of behavior.

Key # 107 - Live your days in serenity, in the midst of seeming chaos.

Key # 108 - By choice and with discipline, the creative life force energy can produce what we call happiness—a path that leads to the greatest treasure—your electromagnetic Light within.

Key # 109 - Through spoken words our thoughts bring about a world of defined results.

Key # 110 - Disciplined activity of monitored thoughts gives us freedom and delivers happiness.

Key # 111 - Contentment is a personal choice, an inner peace.

Key # 112 - Alone or with someone, happiness is a deliberate choice—a discipline acquired by self-control.

Key # 113 - Permanent happiness is virtually impossible for most of us unless we are willing to commit ourselves to self-control and discipline monitored by self-awareness.

Key # 114 - Attitudes of Disdain, Disappointment, Dissatisfaction and Delusion are poison to the sense of happiness and destructive to discipline.

Key # 115 - Suffering is an illness of the ego.

Key # 116 - Experiences of anguish cause an "altered" ego.

Key # 117 - Images are the keys to the invisible world.

Key # 118 - We visualize with our entire being.

Key # 119 - Visualization gives energy to your dream.

Key # 120 - A spirited person is not controlling of others but demonstrates discipline and self-control.

Key # 121 - Use past experiences as stepping-stones to new heights.

Key # 122 - When we choose the key called trust, we can open the door to contentment.

Key # 123 - Emotions are the effect of an experience rather than its cause or origin.

Key # 124 - When we experience a fear we trigger a passion and cause a memorable imprint.

Key # 125 - Anger is a false sense of power, another type of fear that elicits subtle control of others.

Key # 126 - "Selfless service" is another form of fear.

Key # 127 - You are solely responsible for everything that you feel.

Key # 128 - Much of anger and worry are based on labeling.

Key # 129 - Forgiveness comes much more easily when you begin to realize that no one really "did it" to you.

Key # 130 - As children we receive messages from adults that cause us to imprint emotions in our memory banks with messages of shame and guilt.

Key # 131 - Acquire a thirst for knowledge.

Key # 132 - Shame not only destroys the sense of trust in self; it also has an uncanny ability to debilitate one's intuitiveness.

Key # 133 - Dare to trust your intuition for resolving issues.

Key # 134 - Once you place the cornerstone of integrity—integration or wholeness, getting it all together—in the base of electromagnetic energy around your auric field, you have begun to build your castle of nobility.

Key # 135 - As long as you remain trusting with an open mind about life, you will sail freely and have control over your destiny.

Key # 136 - Laughter allows you to release tension from your physical body.

Key # 137 - Joy is not brought to you by another; you bring joy to yourself.

Key # 138 - One of the requirements of self-fulfillment is the ability to gracefully make fun of yourself and feel good about it.

Key # 139 - Your friends are those who can laugh with and not at you.

Key # 140 - The ability to perceive a situation with humor gives you the power to evaluate it with strength.

Key # 141 - Our responsibility lies in having a sense of humor with a profound respect for others.

Key # 142 - Life's vicissitudes can sometimes numb our senses.

Key #143 - Having a sense of humor allows you to view the matter at hand objectively.

Key # 144 - A life full of humor and laughter will be a long one.

Key # 145 - No instruction book can teach you how to develop a sense of humor or change your attitude toward life.

Key # 146 - Seeds of humor will make life fruitful, a growing adventure.

Key # 147 - The very fiber of existence lies in the strength of complementary energies that we all bring into the world.

Key # 148 - Cynicism and hostility toward others create a cesspool that becomes a pit for enthusiasm and humor to stumble into.

Key # 149 - Negative humor, such as sarcasm and cynical remarks elicit negative responses from others.

Key # 150 - Self-respect, self-esteem and self-determination are the seeds of independence and the fruits of sovereignty that allow a person to develop autonomy.

Key # 151 - Independence is the state of resting well-assured upon the centeredness of one's inner light.

Key # 152 - Difficulty in letting go of concern for others is founded in a need or desire to control others.

Key # 153 - Love people as they are, without trying to fix them.

Key # 154 - To become actively involved with what is happening around us includes being receptive.

Key # 155 - When we become more aware of the relationship we have with ourselves we will discover the source of our self-worth.

Key # 156 - Weak relationships with others stem from a weak relationship with ourselves.

Key # 157 - Creating independent relationships requires a sharpened vision that is devoid of co-dependent irregularities.

Key # 158 - Independence doesn't just happen; it happens just.

Key # 159 - Self-esteem and independence are closely tied to family and environment.

Key # 160 - Comparing yourself to others, your former self or your "ideal" self for the purpose of pronouncing "judgments" is a vicious cycle of sabotage.

Key # 161 - Helping others help themselves is a form of self-love and self-worth.

Key # 162 - When relationships have a good "giver" and an uncomfortable "receiver," they become unhealthy and co-dependent.

Key # 163 - A valuable way to stay on track with a plan is to monitor your conscious efforts for 21 days.

Key # 164 - When we go within and allow ourselves to consider our vulnerabilities we become empowered by a sense of dignity.

Key # 165 - Breaking co-dependency can easily be called the invisible new road.

Key # 166 - Gender issues usually lie hidden in a co-dependent relationship.

Key # 167 - A healthy independent relationship develops when a person has a passion for creating one.

Key # 168 - Happiness is a "self-referral" effort.

Key # 169 - In order to develop a secure relationship with yourself it is necessary to become responsible for your own experiences.

Key # 170 - Begin your relationships by communicating your feelings in words that say exactly how you feel.

Key # 171 - Avoid behaviors that bring personal gain.

Key # 172 - The nature of evolution is to progress ourselves toward the ability to self-reflect.

Key # 173 - Success is the product of success.

Key # 174 - Love is the propelling force behind the desire to evolve.

Key # 175 - Our attitude often determines the outcome of a situation.

Key # 176 - Bringing up the past needn't be burdensome.

Key # 177 - Self-fulfillment is attained by the acquisition of certain attributes that build our character.

Key # 178 - Become friends first, and remain friends forever.

Key # 179 - The destination of our life's journey is wisely kept well hidden within us: it's up to us to discover it!

Key # 180 - It is the little things that go undetected that we must become keenly aware of.

Key # 181 - Some voyages may seem more challenging than others.

Key # 182 - The beauty of life lies in the fact that everything reveals itself in time.

Key # 183 - The world is viewed as the observer desires.

Key # 184 - Change is a natural evolutionary process that brings one to self-fulfillment.

Key # 185 - The power of gratitude is magical.

Key # 186 - Self-fulfillment comes decorated with strength of character.

Key # 187 - On our life's journey into forever, we are only voyagers.

Key # 188 - Our integrity is the way we see ourselves as part of the whole picture.

Key # 189 - Self-appreciation for the resource we can be to others is valuable.

Key # 190 - Once you open the channels of your own understanding, you too will feel the rapture of being alive.

Key # 191 - Knowing that life is a process and not a destination, will afford the peace and happiness that comes from self-acceptance.

Key # 192 - To desire a spontaneous result is nothing more than living the natural impulse to create self-fulfillment.

Key # 193 - Love is who we are!

About the Author

Jeanette O'Donnal is a Clinical Hypnotherapist, shaman, master teacher of Ancient Wisdom and life coach, with a Self Realization Center and bookstore in Payson, Arizona. Through carefully positioned questions, she has acquired an uncanny ability to view causes beyond symptoms, intuitively sense the proper course of action and prompt others to find solutions. A mother of seven children and descendent of the great Mayan tradition of wisdom and healing, in this book, O'Donnal combines practical knowledge with an abundance of anecdotes and personal stories.

IF YOU LIKED THIS BOOK, YOU WON'T WANT TO MISS OTHER TITLES BY DANDELION BOOKS

Available Now And Always Through
www.dandelionbooks.net And Affiliated Websites!!

TOLL-FREE ORDERS – 1-800-861-7899 (U.S. & CANADA)

Non-Fiction:

The Courage To Be Who I Am, by Mary-Margareht Rose... This book is rich with teachings and anecdotes delivered with humor and humanness, by a woman who followed her heart and learned to listen to her inner voice; in the process, transforming every obstacle into an opportunity to test her courage to manifest her true identity. (ISBN 1-893302-13-X)

The Clear and Simple Way: The Angel Lessons, by Judith Parsons... a book about heart, with heart. Parsons, known throughout the world for her spiritual workshops and seminars, shows us how to transform our lives into infinite "presents"—"gifts" and moment-by-moment experiences—of peace, joy and self-fulfillment. (ISBN 1-893302-43-1)

Stranger than Fiction: An Independent Investigation Of The True Culprits Behind 9-11, by Albert D. Pastore, Ph.D... Twelve months of careful study, painstaking research, detailed analysis, source verification and logical deduction went into the writing of this book. In addition to the stories are approximately 300 detailed footnotes Pastore: "Only by sifting through huge amounts of news data on a daily basis was I able to catch many of these rare 'diamonds in the rough' and organize them into a coherent pattern and logical argument." (ISBN 1-893302-47-4)

Ahead Of The Parade: A Who's Who Of Treason and High Crimes – Exclusive Details Of Fraud And Corruption Of The Monopoly Press, The Banks, The Bench And The Bar, And The Secret Political Police, by Sherman H. Skolnick... One of America's foremost investigative reporters, speaks out on some of America's current crises. Included in this blockbuster book are

255

the following articles: Big City Newspapers & the Mob, The Sucker Traps, Dirty Tricks of Finance and Brokerage, The Secret History of Airplane Sabotage, Wal-Mart and the Red Chinese Secret Police, The Chandra Levy Affair, The Japanese Mafia in the United States, The Secrets of Timothy McVeigh, and much more. (ISBN 1-893302-32-6)

Palestine & The Middle East: Passion, Power & Politics, by Jaffer Ali... The Palestinian struggle is actually a human one that transcends Palestine... There is no longer a place for Zionism in the 20th century... Democracy in the Middle East is mot safe for US interests as long as there is an atmosphere of hostility... Suicide bombings are acts of desperation and mean that a people have been pushed to the brink... failure to understand why they happen will make certain they will continue. Jaffer Ali is a Palestinian-American business man who has been writing on politics and business for over 25 years. (ISBN 1-893302-45-8)

America, Awake! We Must Take Back Our Country, by Norman D. Livergood... This book is intended as a wake-up call for Americans, as Paul Revere awakened the Lexington patriots to the British attack on April 18, 1775, and as Thomas Paine's *Common Sense* roused apathetic American colonists to recognize and struggle against British oppression. Our current situation is similar to that which American patriots faced in the 1770s: a country ruled by 'foreign' and 'domestic' plutocratic powers and a divided citizenry uncertain of their vital interests. (ISBN 1-893302-27-X)

The Perennial Tradition: Overview Of The Secret Heritage, The Single Stream Of Initiatory Teaching Flowing Through All The Great Schools Of Mysticism, by Norman D. Livergood... Like America, Awake, this book is another wake-up call. "It was written to assist readers to awaken to the Higher Spiritual World." In addition to providing a history of the Western tradition of the Perennial Tradition, Livergood also describes the process that serious students use to actually *realize*—bring to manifestation—their Higher Consciousness. "Unless we become aware of this higher state, we face the prospect of a basically useless physical existence and a future life—following physical death—of unpleasant, perhaps anguished reformation of our essence." (ISBN 1-893302-48-2)

The Awakening of An American: How America Broke My Heart, by Meria Heller, with a Foreword by Catherine Austin Fitts... A collection of choice interviews from Meria Heller's world-famous www.meria.net rapidly growing radio network that reaches millions of people daily. Dr. Arun Gandhi, Greg Palast, Vincent Bugliosi, Mark Elsis, William Rivers Pitt,

Mark Rechtenwald, Nancy Oden & Bob Fertik, Howard Winant, Linda Starr, Dave Chandler, Bev Conover, John Nichols, Robert McChesney, Norman Solomon, Stan Goff and Mark Crispin Miller. (ISBN 1-89302-39-3)

America's Nightmare: The Presidency of George Bush II, by John Stanton & Wayne Madsen... Media & Language, War & Weapons, Internal Affairs and a variety of other issues pointing out the US "crisis without precedent" that was wrought by the US Presidential election of 2000 followed by 9/11. "Stanton & Madsen will challenge many of the things you've been told by CNN and Fox news. This book is dangerous." (ISBN 1-893302-29-6)

America's Autopsy Report, by John Kaminski... The false fabric of history is unraveling beneath an avalanche of pathological lies to justify endless war and Orwellian new laws that revoke the rights of Americans. While TV and newspapers glorify the dangerous ideas of perverted billionaires, the Internet has pulsated with outrage and provided a new and real forum for freedom among concerned people all over the world who are opposed to the mass murder and criminal exploitation of the defenseless victims of multinational corporate totalitarianism. John Kaminski's passionate essays give voice to those hopes and fears of humane people that are ignored by the big business shysters who rule the major media. (ISBN 1-893302-42-3)

Seeds Of Fire: China And The Story Behind The Attack On America, by Gordon Thomas... The inside story about China that no one can afford to ignore. Using his unsurpassed contacts in Israel, Washington, London and Europe, Gordon Thomas, internationally acclaimed best-selling author and investigative reporter for over a quarter-century, reveals information about China's intentions to use the current crisis to launch itself as a super-power and become America's new major enemy...*"This has been kept out of the news agenda because it does not suit certain business interests to have that truth emerge... Every patriotic American should buy and read this book... it is simply revelatory."* (Ray Flynn, Former U.S. Ambassador to the Vatican) (ISBN 1-893302-54-7)

Shaking The Foundations: Coming Of Age In The Postmodern Era, by John H. Brand, D. Min., J.D.... Scientific discoveries in the Twentieth Century require the restructuring of our understanding the nature of Nature and of human beings. In simple language the author explains how significant impli-cations of quantum mechanics, astronomy, biology and brain physiology form the foundation for new perspectives to comprehend the meaning of our lives. (ISBN 1-893302-25-3)

Rebuilding The Foundations: Forging A New And Just America, by John H. Brand, D. Min., J.D.... Should we expect a learned scholar to warn us about our dangerous reptilian brains that are the real cause of today's evils? Although Brand is not without hope for rescuing America, he warns us to act fast–and now. Evil men intent on imposing their political, economic, and religious self-serving goals on America are not far from achieving their goal of mastery." (ISBN 1-893302-33-4)

Democracy Under Siege: The Jesuits' Attempt To Destroy the Popular Government Of The United States; The True Story of Abraham Lincoln's Death; Banned For Over 100 Years, This Information Now Revealed For The First Time! by C.T. Wilcox... U.S. President Lincoln was the triumphant embodiment of the New Concept of Popular Government. Was John Wilkes Booth a Jesuit patsy, hired to do the dirty work for the Roman Catholic church – whose plan, a well-kept secret until now – was to overthrow the American Government? (ISBN 1-893302-31-8)

The Last Atlantis Book You'll Ever Have To Read! by Gene D. Matlock... More than 25,000 books, plus countless other articles have been written about a fabled confederation of city-states known as Atlantis. If it really did exist, where was it located? Does anyone have valid evidence of its existence – artifacts and other remnants? According to historian, archaeologist, educator and linguist Gene D. Matlock, both questions can easily be answered. (ISBN 1-893302-20-2)

The Last Days Of Israel, by Barry Chamish... With the Middle East crisis ongoing, *The Last Days of Israel* takes on even greater significance as an important book of our age. Barry Chamish, investigative reporter who has the true story about Yitzak Rabin's assassination, tells it like it is. (ISBN 1-893302-16-4)

Fiction:

Freedom: Letting Go Of Anxiety And Fear Of The Unknown, by Jim Britt... Jeremy Carter, a fireman from Missouri who is in New York City for the day, decides to take a tour of the Trade Center, only to watch in shock, the attack on its twin towers from a block away. Afterward as he gazes at the pit of rubble and talks with many of the survivors, Jeremy starts to explore the inner depths of his soul, to ask questions he'd never asked before. This dialogue helps him learn who he is and what it takes to overcome the fear, anger, grief and anxiety this kind of tragedy brings. (ISBN 1-893302-74-1)

Synchronicity Gates: An Anthology Of Stories And Poetry About People Transformed In Extraordinary Reality Beyond Experience, by Stephen Vernarelli... An inventive compilation of short stories that take the reader beyond mere science, fiction, or fantasy. Vernarelli introduces the reader to a new perception of reality; he imagines the best and makes it real. (ISBN 1-893302-38-5)

The Alley of Wishes, by Laurel Johnson... Despite the ravages of WWI on Paris and on the young American farm boy, Beck Sanow, and despite the abusive relationship that the chanteuse Cerise endures, the two share a bond that is unbreakable by time, war, loss of memory, loss of life and loss of youth. Beck and Cerise are both good people beset by constant tragedy. Yet it is tragedy that brings them together, and it is unconditional love that keeps them together. (ISBN 1-893302-46-6)

The Prince Must Die, by Gower Leconfield... breaks all taboos for mystery thrillers. After the "powers that be" suppressed the manuscripts of three major British writers, Dandelion Books breaks through with a thriller involving a plot to assassinate Prince Charles. *The Prince Must Die* brings to life a Britain of today that is on the edge with race riots, neo-Nazis, hard right backlash and neo-punk nihilists. Riveting entertainment... you won't be able to put it down. (ISBN 1-893302-72-5)

Waaaay Out There! Diggertown, Oklahoma, by Tuklo Nashoba... Adventures of constable Clint Mankiller and his deputy, Chad GhostWolf; Jim Bob and Bubba Johnson, Grandfather GhostWolf, Cassie Snodgrass, Doc Jones, Judge Jenkins and the rest of the Diggertown, Oklahoma bunch in the first of a series of Big Foot-Sasquatch tall tales peppered with lots of good belly laughs and just as much fun. (ISBN 1-893302-44-X)

Daniela, by Stephen Weeks... A gripping epic novel of sexual obsession and betrayal as Nazi Prague falls. The harboring of deadly secrets and triumph of an enduring love against the hardest of times. Nikolei is a Polish/Ukrainian Jew who finds himself fighting among the Germans then turning against them to save Prague in 1945. Nikolei manages to hide himself among the Germans with a woman working as a prostitute. (ISBN 1-893302-37-7)

Unfinished Business, by Elizabeth Lucas Taylor... Lindsay Mayer knows something is amiss when her husband, Griffin, a college professor, starts spending too much time at his office and out-of-town. Shortly after the ugly truth surfaces, Griffin disappears altogether. Lindsay is shattered. Life without

Griffin is life without life... One of the sexiest books you'll ever read! (ISBN 1-893302-68-7)

The Woman With Qualities, by Sarah Daniels... South Florida isn't exactly the Promised Land that forty-nine-year-old newly widowed Keri Anders had in mind when she transplanted herself here from the northeast... A tough action-packed novel that is far more than a love story. (ISBN 1-893302-11-3)

Weapon In Heaven, by David Bulley... Eddy Licklighter is in a fight with God for his very own soul. You can't mess around half-assed when fighting with God. You've got to go at it whole-hearted. Eddy loses his wife and baby girl in a fire. Bulley's protagonist is a contemporary version of the Old Testament character of Job. Licklighter wants nothing from God except His presence so he can kill him off. The humor, warmth, pathos and ultimate redemption of Licklighter will make you hold your sides with laughter at the same time you shed common tears for his "God-awful" dilemma. (ISBN 1-893302-28-8)

Adventure Capital, by John Rushing... South Florida adventure, crime and violence in a fiction story based on a true life experience. A book you will not want to put down until you reach the last page. (ISBN 1-893302-08-3)

A Mother's Journey: To Release Sorrow And Reap Joy, by Sharon Kay... A poignant account of Norah Ann Mason's life journey as a wife, mother and single parent. This book will have a powerful impact on anyone, female or male, who has experienced parental abuse, family separations, financial struggles and a desperate need to find the magic in life that others talk about that just doesn't seem to be there for them. (ISBN 1-893302-52-0)

Return To Masada, by Robert G. Makin... In a gripping account of the famous Battle of Masada, Robert G. Makin skillfully recaptures the blood and gore as well as the spiritual essence of this historic struggle for freedom and independence. (ISBN 1-893302-10-5)

Time Out Of Mind, by Solara Vayanian... Atlantis had become a snake pit of intrigue teeming with factious groups vying for power and control. An unforgettable drama that tells of the breakdown of the priesthood, the hidden scientific experiments in genetic engineering which produced "things"—part human and part animal—and other atrocities; the infiltration by the dark lords of Orion; and the implantation of the human body with a device to fuel the Orion wars. (ISBN 1-893302-21-0)

The Thirteenth Disciple: The Life Of Mary Magdalene, by Gordon Thomas... The closest of Jesus' followers, the name of Mary Magdalene conjures images of a woman both passionate and devoted, both sinner and saint. The first full-length biography for 13 centuries. (ISBN 1-893302-17-2)

ALL DANDELION BOOKS ARE AVAILABLE THROUGH WWW.DANDELIONBOOKS.NET... ALWAYS.